A Study in Woodlands Archaeology: Cudham, North Downs

Sue Harrington

BAR British Series 368
2004

Published in 2016 by
BAR Publishing, Oxford

BAR British Series 368

A Study in Woodlands Archaeology: Cudham, North Downs

ISBN 978 1 84171 601 5

BAR Publishing is the trading name of British Archaeological Reports (Oxford) Ltd.
British Archaeological Reports was first incorporated in 1974 to publish the BAR
Series, International and British. In 1992 Hadrian Books Ltd became part of the BAR
group. This volume was originally published by Archaeopress in conjunction with
British Archaeological Reports (Oxford) Ltd / Hadrian Books Ltd, the Series principal
publisher, in 2004. This present volume is published by BAR Publishing, 2016.

Printed in England

BAR
PUBLISHING

BAR titles are available from:

BAR Publishing
122 Banbury Rd, Oxford, OX2 7BP, UK
EMAIL   info@barpublishing.com
PHONE   +44 (0)1865 310431
FAX   +44 (0)1865 316916
www.barpublishing.com

In memory of
JOHN HARRINGTON
1910 -1994

ACKNOWLEDGEMENTS

This study is a revision of my undergraduate thesis, carried out at the Institute of Archaeology, University College, London in 1997. The initial project was supervised by Gustav Milne and was extended and prepared for publication under the editorial guidance of Jon Hather. Alister Hayes, Countryside Officer, first brought to my attention the wealth of woodland landscape extant within the London Borough of Bromley and shared his detailed local knowledge. Paul Cullen, of the Institute of Name-Studies, School of English Studies, University of Nottingham gave an invaluable commentary on the place-name evidence and the content of appendix 2. Grateful thanks are offered to each of these for their support and advice.

Practical support in the field, surveying the woodbanks and recording the trees, was given by Jo Birch, Liz Evans, Kate Hall, Kath Craw, Teresa Sharpe, Sarah Humphries and Tina Stevens, all of whose interested conversation and enthusiasm made this project possible. Special thanks to Lea Myers for her continued support throughout the project.

Thanks are also due to Mr Dimbleby of Norsted Manor Farm, Mr Hick of New Barn Farm and Mr Kirby of Skid Hill Farm for permission to survey on their lands; Mrs Wells for information on the yews in Cudham churchyard; Mary Gander for her report on the restoration of Cudham church; the staff of Bromley Local Studies Library; the staff of the County Record Office, Maidstone, Kent.

Although in hindsight some of the original propositions that were explored and the methods used now appear to be simplistic, it is hoped that this research will eventually provide the basis for an in-depth whole parish study that will more fully explore this fascinating landscape.

ABSTRACT

The woodland banking in the parish of Cudham on the North Downs was examined to establish the phases of expansion and contraction of the woodlands in the Medieval period. An anomaly was evident between the Domesday Book reference suggesting extensive ploughlands and a post-Medieval reference suggesting extensive woodlands. Synthesis of the evidence from a sampling survey of the banking, the place-name evidence and from documentary sources suggested changes in the land use and settlement patterns, with the woodlands consistently prominent through all periods. The extant banking is thought to relate to the earliest Medieval settlement of the parish, which probably took the form of bounded estates. Their later use as woodland banks has preserved them in the landscape. Early Medieval use of the landscape for transhumant pasturing, followed by a dispersed settlement in the woodlands, led to a limited, arable, open field system in the later Medieval period. Non-manorial land tenure was characterised by renting, indicating the ability to generate income through the sale of surplus woodland products. The post-Medieval period is characterised by privately-owned woodland compartments. The conclusion is drawn that, over time, Cudham has been maintained as a specialised, woodland resource producing area in the hinterland of London.

TABLE OF CONTENTS

LIST OF FIGURES

LIST OF PHOTOS, with locations and grid references

SUE HARRINGTON

INTRODUCTION

For the people of south London in the early twenty-first century, seeking a Sunday afternoon stroll away from the housing estates and suburban sprawl of the metropolis, the North Downs are our closest area of open countryside (see location map, fig.1). The Downs have latterly become firmly fixed within the orbit of London by the arc of the M25 motorway and their designation, in part, as the southernmost boundary of Greater London. Scattered with woodlands, fields and steep, twisting lanes, this Downland landscape has, however, changed considerably in the past twenty years, designation as Green Belt notwithstanding. Swathes of countryside have been transformed for recreational purposes, as golf courses and garden centres, for new roads and for commuter housing, purposes that have in the main been dictated by the economic and social demands of London. Yet, visible from the lanes and the networks of bridle and footpaths that criss-cross the Downs, are aspects of a much older landscape, hinted at also by place-names of Anglo-Saxon origin, perhaps indicating an earlier life independent of London.

The Lower Thames basin as a whole is fringed with what were once predominantly wooded areas, such as the Chiltern Hills, the North Downs and South West Essex (Peterken, 1993). The London borough of Bromley contains 32% of the ancient woodlands still extant within the Greater London area, that is, those originating before AD1600, much of it now in private ownership or managed for public recreation (Hayes, 1994). Ancient, wooded, common lands, such as at Hayes in Bromley, together with bounded parks such as that of Scadbury Manor in Chislehurst, are to be found on the dip-slope of the North Downs. On the Downs proper, however, are the remains of a more extensive system of anciently managed woodland. This is evidenced by stretches of woodbanks, those Medieval earthworks that surrounded or subdivided a wood, together with trees that demonstrate a history of systematic management. In the London borough of Bromley, the majority of these woodbanks occur in the southernmost parish of Cudham (Hayes, 1994). Parts of the Cudham landscape appear to be recently fashioned from cleared woodland, however, particularly along the A233 road from Keston to Westerham. With regular boundaries and single-species hedgerows, the fields on top of the Downs adjacent to this road appear as products of landscape pattern formed in the nineteenth century. This perception is supported by the absence, within the parish, of those nucleated villages of Medieval timber framed houses and the sinuous field boundaries that are prevalent further south into Kent and the Weald. Indeed, the absence of any settlement nucleation, before the development of commuter housing in the early twentieth century, is particularly noticeable.

Yet, on place-name evidence, Cudham is a long settled area within the landscape of the Downs, extant before the Norman Conquest of AD1066. W. G. Hoskins, in his seminal work *The Making of the English Landscape*, asserts that 'The English landscape itself, to those who know how to read it aright, is the richest historical document we possess' (1955:14). For Tom Williamson and Liz Bellamy, the landscape is an explicitly social document, commenting that 'the fabric of the landscape gives a particular insight into the communities that have lived and worked within it, and above all it embodies a history of power in the land' (1987:9). Implicit within these comments is the idea that the landscape is not solely nature being worked upon, but is a unique human creation that has changed over time, that can be traced and analysed through archaeological and historical research.

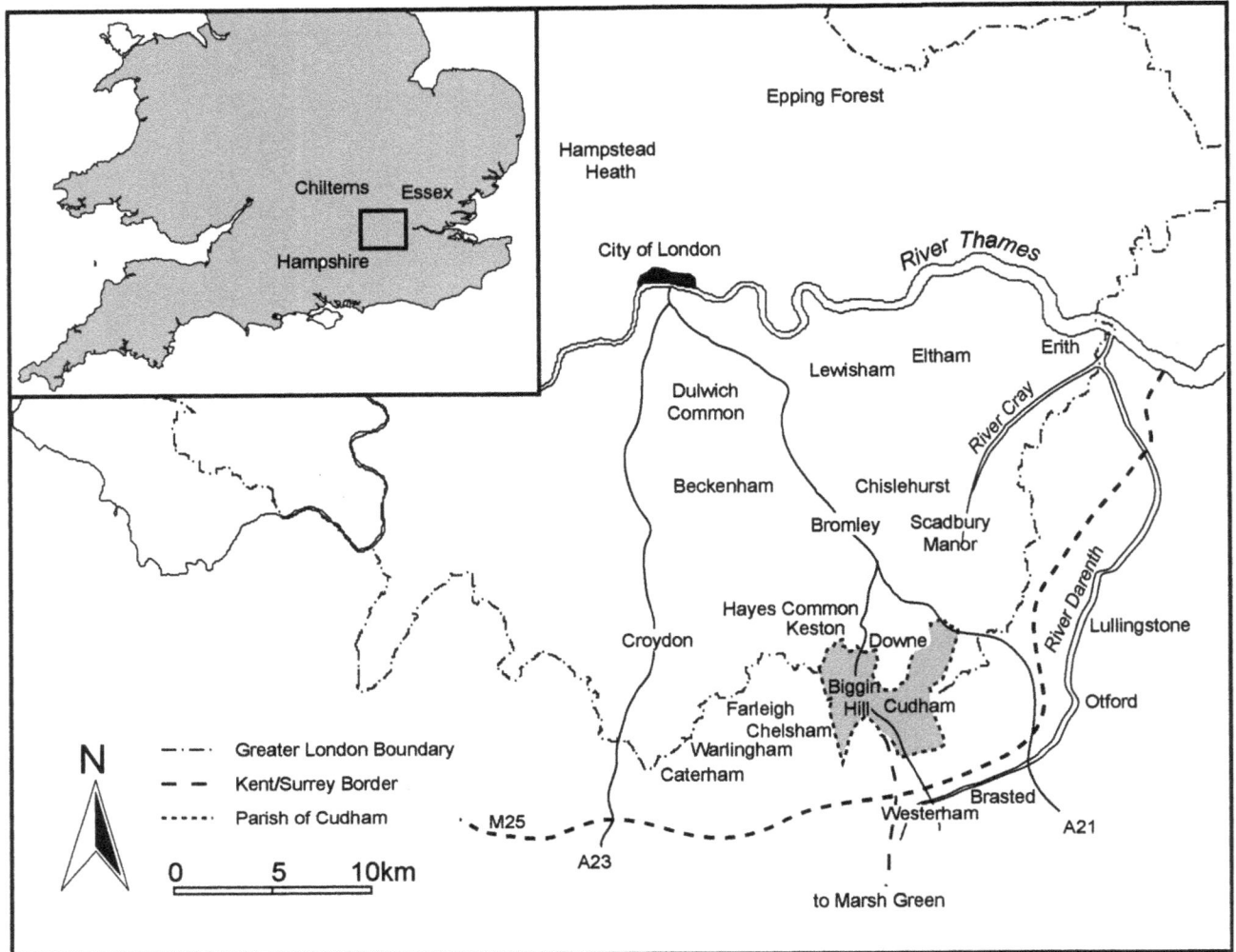

Fɪɢᴜʀᴇ 1. Lᴏᴄᴀᴛɪᴏɴ ᴍᴀᴘ ᴏꜰ Cᴜᴅʜᴀᴍ ɪɴ Gʀᴇᴀᴛᴇʀ Lᴏɴᴅᴏɴ.

The question arises whether the North Downs, and Cudham in particular, have been enduringly impacted by the economic and social demands of London and at what point that impact may have begun to manifest itself in the patterns of the landscape. As a preliminary explanatory proposition, it can be suggested that the North Downs have acted as a peripheral, principally woodland, resource for London's urban core, in a model that mirrors the physical relationship of the Downs to London. This model suggests that when economic power is geographically centred, that is, when it has a discernible spatial patterning, there is also an inherent relationship of unequal exchange. As a result the peripheral places 'remain underdeveloped for lack of access to their own surplus' and the net benefits flow to the centre (Cater and Jones, 1989:20). Once places are fixed in this system of unequal interdependence, the periphery loses the ability to transform its economic position. This situation impacts also on local social relations. For example, in modern societies, a primary effect of industrialisation has been to undermine agriculture as a source of rural employment, leading to rural depopulation and a concentration of landownership into fewer hands. In feudal communities, such as probably existed in Cudham, this subordinate position in relation to the expanding urban core, facilitated a rigid social hierarchy wherein the surplus products of the dispersed rural peasantry were expropriated by a hereditary land-owning elite (Cater and Jones, 1989:197).

This core/periphery model, generated in the main by modern social geographers, works most clearly when dealing with the spatial impacts of modern industrial capitalism. Yet, as Matthew Johnson (1996:38) notes 'The early modern period saw ... changes (which) created the preconditions for large scale urbanisation and industrialisation in the second half of the eighteenth century' and that the 'key arena of social and cultural transformation' was the pre-industrial countryside. The period AD1400 - 1750 has been characterised as part of the Feudal/Capitalist Transition (Johnson, 1996:4). This perspective emphasises the commodification of the landscape over time, wherein the rights and customs of access to resources were replaced by the ability to purchase within a money-based economy.

If the landscape is a document on which the cultural changes of the past have been incised and if Cudham is inextricably linked to the growth of London, as an urban centre dominating its hinterland, then research into the parish might comment on the earliest phases of the core/periphery model. Documentary evidence for the parish hints, however, at a greater complexity. Cudham is mentioned in the Domesday Book of AD1086. The entry refers to ten ploughs, indicating a labour intensive system of arable agriculture that is usually associated with nucleated settlements (Steane, 1984:145). The dominant perception of the Downs in this period, however, is that they were sparsely settled and covered in woodland (Darby, 1951). The Domesday Book reference suggests, therefore, that Cudham was as area of arable production as early as the eleventh century. This contrasts with the situation in the nineteenth century when 'Cudham Woods stretched intact for over two miles through the heart of the parish' (Thorne, 1876:4, referring to the landscape of fifty years earlier). By this period, many tracts of woodland elsewhere in lowland England had been systematically cleared for arable farming, as a consequence of the Agricultural Revolution in the eighteenth century. This last cited reference suggests a re-wooding of Cudham parish, in the later and post-Medieval periods, perhaps in response to demand for woodland products in London. These woodlands in the heart of the parish were cleared, in the latter part of the nineteenth century, for cornfields and for market gardens, supplying soft fruit to London, in a further working out of the core/periphery model. In the twentieth century all remnants of these woodlands were covered by the airfield and the Second World war fighter base at Biggin Hill.

METHODOLOGY

In order to engage with the complexity of the changing importance of woodland to the economy of Cudham in the historic period, a research project was devised using the methods and techniques of woodlands archaeology. A distinction is made here between archaeology in woodland and the archaeology of woodland. The former deals with archaeological remains that are now situated within woods, for example farmsteads, burial mounds, kilns and ridge and furrow, that is, those features that are not directly related to woodland use but that have become subsumed within them. The archaeology of woodlands, hereafter termed woodlands archaeology, deals with features that relate specifically to woodland management. These include woodbanks, charcoal pits, saw pits, living structures, such as managed trees, and areas that are wooded, such as shaws and plantations. As a relatively new sub-discipline of landscape archaeology, woodlands archaeology's full potential has not, as yet, been realised. It fits most readily, at present, within the theoretical perspectives of economic and environmental determinism, that give a prime role to key staples, such as woodland products, in considerations of social change in the past.

Woodbanks are of particular significance, as they are earthworks that remain visible even when the woods have been cleared in later phases of land use. Oliver Rackham (1986:36) states that '…woodbanks have meanings. They record the histories of woods in ways which complement written records. Unlike most documents, woodbanks are precise as to place but vague as to date'. In addition, they represent a labour investment of in the region of 5000 hours per mile of the largest banking (Rackham, 1986:39), with the assumed purpose of defining and defending the woodland and to prevent the ingress of deer. Rackham indicates that mapped reconstructions of woods are possible through detailed fieldwork, for example in The Woods of South East Essex. Peterken (1993:206-10) outlines fieldwork methods for woodland archaeology that include walking the linear features and noting their distinctive forms, noting tree species distribution and forms, and soil types. Other strands of evidence might also be sought, particularly from map and documentary evidence, in order to achieve a synthesis of information wherein no one dataset has hegemony.

For the purposes of this study, which analyses the archaeological remains of woodlands, it was important to establish a context for them as a resource over time, with a particular emphasis on their social, economic and political importance in the Medieval period (AD450-1550). A literature review of detailed local studies into changing patterns of woodland use in the Medieval period is therefore included in this research report.

Cudham had not been the subject of detailed historical research, therefore a summary of published historical sources was generated and discussed to add to the contextual framework, with particular consideration of the Domesday Book entry. Archaeological data relating to Cudham and its environs was gathered together, in order to identify elements of continuity and change from the prehistoric period. Environmental evidence, including the geological characteristics of the area, was considered, to assess whether this may have had a determining effect on land use. This range of activities facilitated the location of the archaeological evidence of woodlands in Cudham within a wider, temporal and dynamic context.

Whilst this was straightforward in theory, the practical difficulties of woodlands archaeology became apparent very quickly. In order to plan out the methodology for a single season of fieldwork, a pilot study visit to Cudham was carried out in September 1996. The main footpaths and bridlepaths were followed by bicycle, using as a guide the latest Ordnance Survey maps (Pathfinder 1192 and 1208, 1:25000, 1989). It became clear that it would be unrealistic to record by survey all of the banks due to the large (5925 acre) size of the parish. Much of the land is in private ownership, with some woods reserved for pheasant shooting. Dense undergrowth presented another hazard, indicating that the winter months would provide optimum access. The banks with associated hedgerows, pollards, standards and coppices were fragmented and intercut by later features, such as flint quarries. Whilst arable and pasture predominate current land use, ploughed out wood banks were visible in the fields, particularly on steep hillsides, indicating that modern, non-woodland areas needed to be included in the study. Examination of aerial photographs allowed the physical links between lengths of banking to be reconstructed.

With these limitations in mind, it was decided to concentrate on a sampling strategy. The Ordnance Survey map indicated that the parish could be split into four discrete areas. These divisions were based on routes cutting through the Downs, which, if themselves ancient, readily marked a coherence to the landscape that had been imposed in an earlier period. These areas are shown on the woodlands map (fig.2) and are identified as follows:

Area 1 (A1) The parish to the west of the road running from Keston to Tatsfield (A233, continuing as a minor road to Tatsfield) and including the Biggin Hill Valley and woods 1-6.

Area 2 (A2) The parish to the east of the road running from Keston to Tatsfield, as far as Berry's Green, suggested as being the extent of Cudham Lodge Wood, and including woods 7-8

Area 3 (A3) The parish to the east of Berry's Green and south of the church, including woods 9-13

Area 4 (A4) The parish north of the church, including woods 14-20

An accessible sector within each area was selected for detailed scrutiny. The nature of the parish boundary banking was also considered, particularly where it divided woodlands from those of a neighbouring parish, as, for example, at woods 21 and 23. Access points to the woods were also sought. That there was a relationship between the banking systems, the trackways and the underlying geology had already been noted (pers. comm. Alister Hayes, Countryside Officer, Bromley Council). The recording method was through the profiling of banks and any associated ditches and tracks, using right angle offsets, in order to establish a local typology. Rackham (1986:36-7) noted that earlier woodbanks tend to be significantly larger than later ones. It was envisaged that similarities with banks found in East Anglia by Rackham could not necessarily be assumed and would need to be demonstrated, before a regional typology for the areas surrounding the lower Thames estuary could be asserted.

The fieldwork for this research project was based around surveys that were non-intrusive. Lengths of extant banking were annotated onto the 1871 Ordnance Survey 6 inch field map (Kent sheet no. 27). Details of trees that had been humanly managed were also

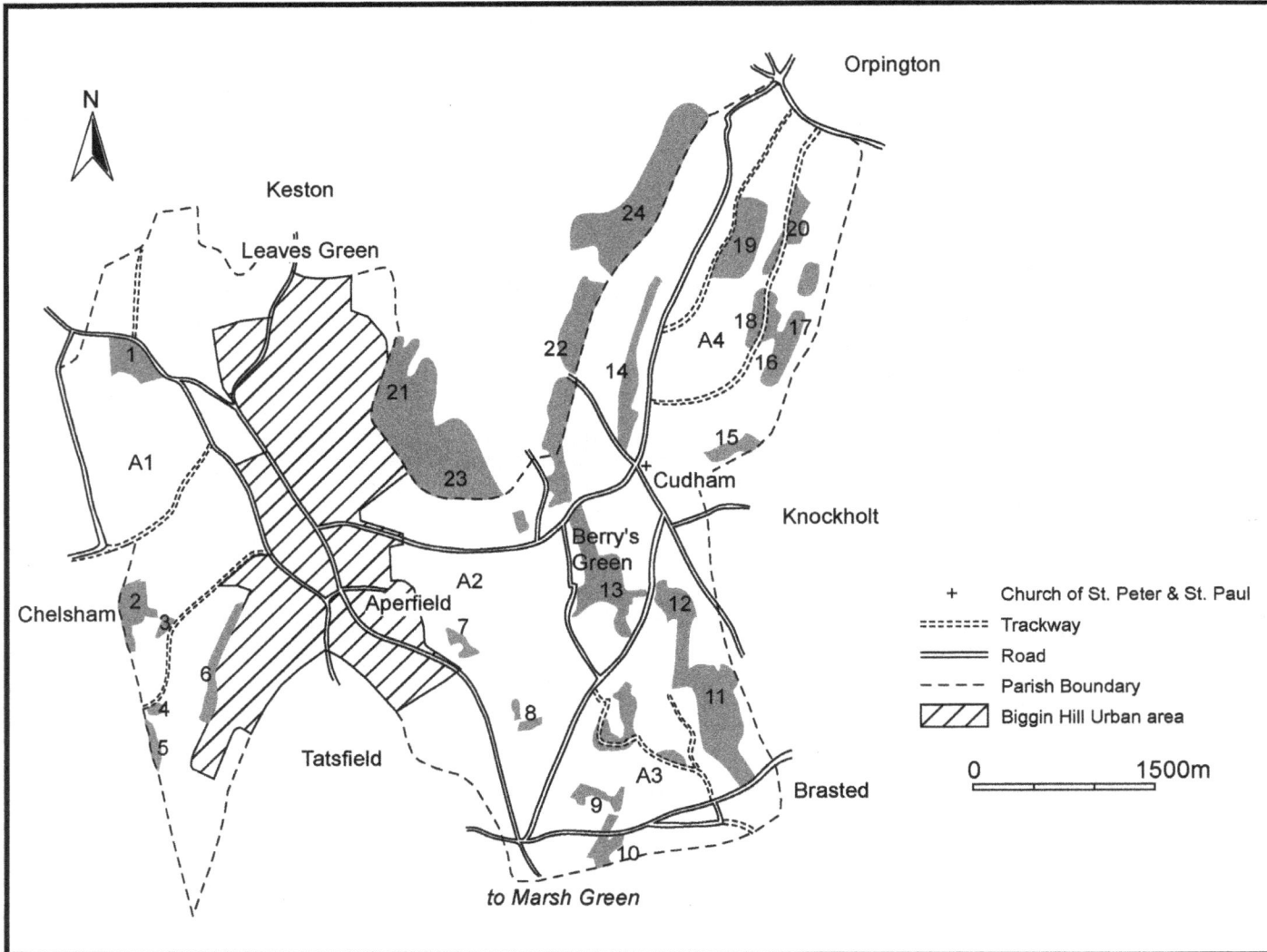

FIGURE 2. THE WOODLANDS OF CUDHAM

1	Jew Jewels Wood	13	Blackbush Shaw
2	Mollards Wood	14	Hazel Wood
3	Jerry Ridden Grove	15	Foxburrow Wood
4	Round Wood	16	Broom Wood
5	Cherry Tree Shaw	17	Homefield Spring
6	Long Coppice	18	Foxberry Wood
7	Pimlico Wood	19	Great molloms Wood
8	Withins Wood	20	Little Molloms Wood
9	Buckhurst	21	Sow Wood
10	Broomcocks Wood	22	Hang Grove
11	Cudham Frith	23	Leasons Wood
12	The Grove Blackbush Shaw	24	Cuckoo Wood

recorded, with regard to species and girth, the latter dimension indicative of age (Mitchell, 1978:25, see also Tree Recording Sheet, Appendix 1). Practical field methods were developed to suit the particular constraints of the locality. Taylor (1974:26) advises against too narrow a focus when examining landscapes and suggests the recording of all features found in the field, in order to build a complete history of a landscape. This approach was particularly valid given the strategic nature of the Biggin Hill airfield in two World Wars. These had necessitated the construction of defensive earthworks throughout the parish, for example banks and ditches around the airfield perimeter, with the additional hazard of bomb craters that were misinterpretable in the field as flint quarries. Linear inspections were carried out along footpaths to address specific questions. An example of this was to consider the changing form of the parish boundary banking where it runs through woodland shared with the adjacent parish, a boundary that had probably been established by the late twelfth century AD (Steane, 1984:151).

Maps and place-name evidence formed a crucial part of this study. The 1871 6 inch Ordnance Survey map predated all of the modern development in the parish and therefore was ideal for use as the main field reference map. The Tithe map of 1838 was consulted for place-name evidence, particularly those field names relating to woodlands. The production of phased land-use maps from a synthesis of all the data, including the documentary evidence, allowed changes to the woodlands within the parish of Cudham to be interpreted in light of the research issues.

THE CULTURAL CREATION OF THE WOODSCAPE

The woodlands present in the English landscape of the early twentyfirst century are the remnants of the changing patterns of human usage of this natural resource. At the beginning of the present post-glacial period, the British Isles were covered in moorland and tundra. As climatic conditions became more favourable, this landscape was progressively colonised from the south by different species of trees, such as birch, pine and willow, followed by lime, hornbeam and oak. Clear regional zones of tree species are evident by 4500BC, based on analyses of archaeologically recovered pollen. Oak and hazel were prevalent in the north and west of Britain, with lime more dominant in the southern areas. Oliver Rackham (1995a:27) has called these prehistoric forests 'wildwood'. That the peoples of the Mesolithic period, who in the main followed a seasonally nomadic, foraging system of subsistence, used the woodlands as a renewable resource is becoming increasingly evident from archaeological research. Pedersen (1995:75-86), for example, discusses fishing structures made from wood and found on waterlogged Danish sites that date to 6320 before present. She intimates that particular species and sizes of material were actively selected for use, possibly from a pre-determined and managed source.

In Britain the patchwork of tree communities became depleted as Neolithic farmers (c.4500-2400BC) cleared the woodlands for cultivation and the pasturing of livestock. This was an uneven process, in that widespread clearance of woodland in the south-east of the British Isles was achieved by c.1800BC, whilst the Highland zone had more localised activity that prolonged the felling until c.600BC (Peterken, 1993:9). Changes to the soil as the result of human activity inhibited woodland regeneration in some areas and caused the formation of lowland heaths, such as that at Bagshot in Surrey. Nevertheless some areas of wildwood remained, and have been termed by Peterken (1993:11) as 'primary' woodland, with those sites which regenerated after an abandonment of agriculture, often with different tree communities, termed as 'secondary' woodland.

The clearance of the landscape for farming, using stone axes, included

small, temporary clearances and larger, permanent clearances ... (with)... the area of the Chalk in southern and eastern England ... being an area of large clearings (Megaw and Simpson, 1979:15).

Sporadic felling of woodlands may have developed into a more definable management strategy from perhaps c.3000BC (Aston,1985:150). Whilst this early management is not evidenced clearly in surviving landscape patterns, the archaeological record does show significant sites where vast quantities of woodland resources were used over time, in a volume beyond which might be expected from the clear felling of the wildwood alone. The thin wooden rods of the woven panels used for the trackways of the Somerset Levels, for example, demonstrate systematic cropping of material from regenerating tree stumps 5000 years ago (Morgan, 1988). Rackham (1977) suggests that poles were more likely a secondary product in the management of coppice for leafy fodder.

John Coles (1978:147-8) suggests, in relation to the Somerset Levels, that resource management in the Neolithic was related to topography, and produced a 'concave landscape', reproduced schematically as fig.3. Here, various areas had different uses, with woodlands generally existing on the uplands, distant from the main areas of settlement, but with some woods that supplied domestic staples, such as firewood and small sized material, being more easily accessible. The form of the managed woodland was, Coles suggests

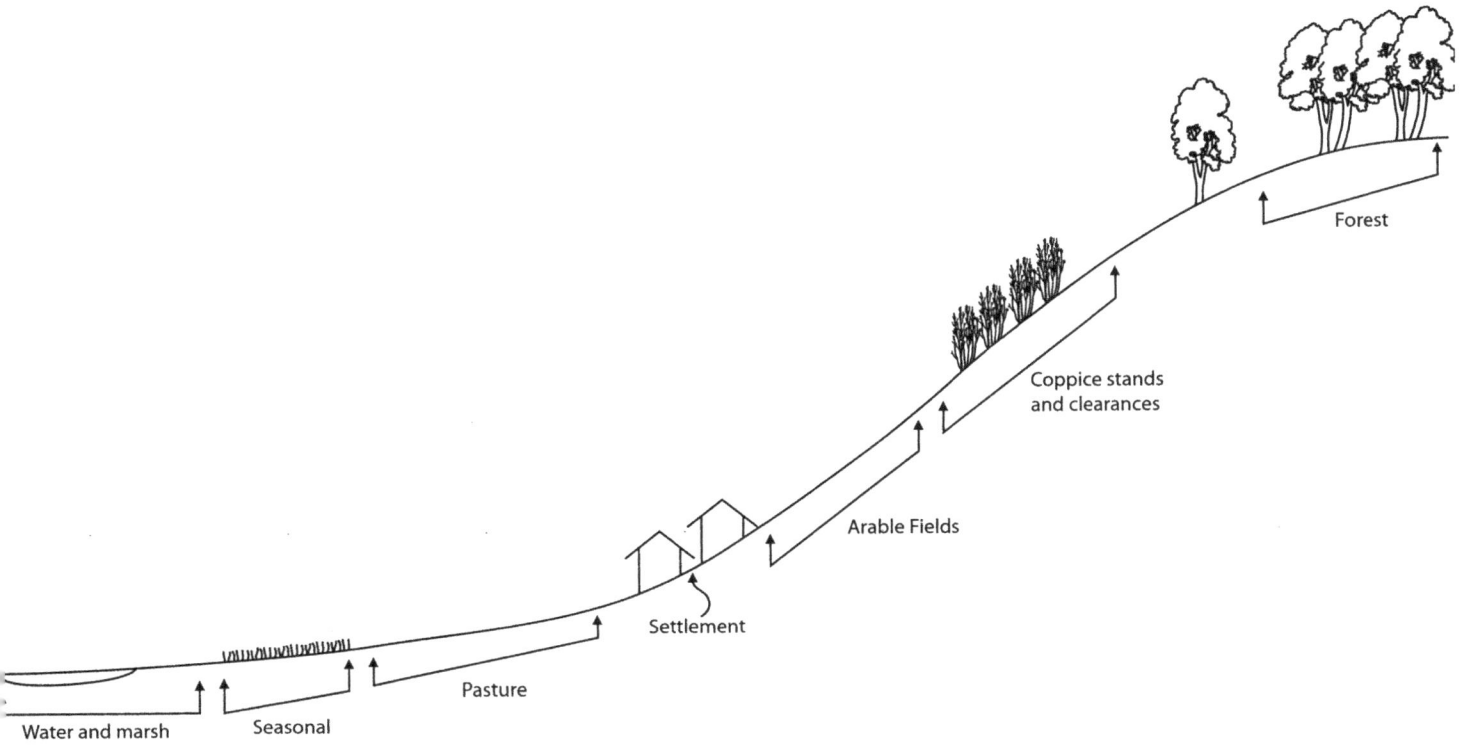

FIGURE 3. A CONCAVE LANDSCAPE

Forest

Coppice stands
and clearances

Arable Fields

Settlement

Pasture

Water and marsh   Seasonal

(1978:148), that of coppice with standards. Coppiced trees are ones that have been cut near to the ground. The stumps, or stools, have the root system and resources of a mature tree and can therefore regenerate rapidly, to produce a stock of rods and poles that can be cropped on a cyclical rotation. The pollarding of trees, wherein the trunk is left to a height of approximately 2 metres but the trunk branches above this are removed, similarly produces a crop of rods and poles. These are beyond the reach of both grazing animals and people. Standards are trees that are left to grow to maturity. These can provide large section (over 60cm in diameter) material when felled, used, for example, to make load bearing structures or monumental edifices. In later periods the standards were predominantly oak, probably due to the durability and strength of this tree species as a construction material when felled. The practice of combining two tree forms to produce different types of woodland crop within the same parcel of land has continued into modern times, perhaps indicative of continual pressure on resource space for the people using the landscape.

The Bronze Age ritual alignments and platforms of Flag Fen, Cambridgeshire, (dated from about 1350BC-950BC) further illustrate the scale of woodland resource production in Antiquity. They are estimated to comprise 4 million pieces of now waterlogged wood (Pryor, 1991), with species such as oak, hazel and alder, of particular forms and sizes indicating that they had been selected for use, possibly from managed resources.

When considering land use patterns, the division of the British Isles into highland and lowland zones, with specific tree species prominent in each (Rackham 1995a:29), has perhaps been too readily derived from a standpoint of environmental determinism. The perceived dominance of pastoralism in the highland zone and arable farming in the lowland zone is challenged by Martin Millett when discussing Late Pre-Roman Iron Age societies. He remarks (1992:10) that 'recent research demonstrates that mixed agriculture was normal throughout the island, but with marked regional variations in micro-climate and topography determining the precise exploitation strategies. This resulted in considerable regional variations within the archaeological data'.

As an example, Millett notes an increase in sheep grazing on the chalk uplands of Wessex, in the lowland area, in this period (1992:10). Barry Cunliffe (1991:378) suggests that '... during the first millennium (BC) massive and concentrated programmes of land clearance and distribution were undertaken ...' with areas such as the clay-with-flints capping the chalk downlands already being exploited by the Middle Iron Age (c.400BC). This is evidenced in the landscape around the Iron Age hill enclosure at Danebury, Hampshire, with land ownership boundaries demarcated by linear earthwork systems.

Peter Reynolds (discussed by Aston, 1985:109) has shown that 20 acres of woodland, within a total holding of 130 acres, was required by a single Iron Age farmstead c.300BC to provide its fuel and building needs. Aston (1985:150) indicates that by this period the extent of wooded areas was already significantly depleted. He suggests that only managed woodland was in existence, although this is difficult to accurately locate and quantify within a given area. Perhaps what is envisaged here is an allocation of woodlands according to social custom, for example for hunting, rather than a direct management of all wooded areas.

Oliver Rackham (1995a:40) concurs that the wildwood had long disappeared by the time the Romans invaded Britain in AD43. Nevertheless, there were sufficient quantities of accessible standing timber to provide the baulks for large scale construction projects, such as the Thames waterfront for the new settlement and port of Londinium, laid down between AD70 and 80 (Milne, 1995:53). Woodland management was an important part of the Romanisation of the landscape, organised to supply building and industrial needs, for example the coppice charcoal to fuel the military ironworks of the Weald (Rackham, 1995a:41). Rackham comments that woods in Roman Britain were mixed coppices, with geological areas such as the chalklands having little or no woodland. Millett notes (1992:02) an increase in the use of woodland for pannage, or the seasonal pasturing of swine, and for hunting in the late Roman period.

The extent to which England was wooded in the mid-fifth century is the subject of conjecture. The departure of the Roman troops in AD410, perhaps signifying the breakdown of centralised government, may have caused the abandonment of the large villa estates, which then reverted to scrub and woodland. The incoming Anglo-Saxons may then have colonised the landscape with piecemeal but vigorous clearing of the woodlands, and imposed the patterns of fields, tracks and settlements that were still discernible in the twenty-first century (Hoskins, 1955). Rackham counters this image by suggesting a degree of continuity with the Roman landscape (1995b:84), wherein areas of extant coppice would have been distinctive and immediately apparent to new settlers. Existing landscape arrangements may have been accepted by the incoming Angles, Saxons and Jutes, and new clearings within woodlands were perhaps a localised, rather than a widespread and pervasive, phenomenon. This view is supported by the regional studies of pre-Conquest woodlands carried out by Della Hooke (1989) in the West Midlands and Alan Everitt (1986) in Kent.

The social importance of woodlands extended beyond the subsistence level of providing staple raw materials for these early communities of settlers and their native British co-habitants. At the local level, woodlands and trees were integral to their concepts of place, evidenced particularly by the processes of naming. Anglo-Saxon charters, delineating parish and estate boundaries, give specific woods and even individual trees as marker points, implying a permanence of the landscape pattern. Old English words associated with the woodland environment have survived in place-names local to Cudham, for example, Chislehurst, meaning 'gravel wooded hill' and Bromley, meaning 'broom clearing' (Gelling, 1993). These names indicate clearings formed within the woodlands for settlement and farming purposes. Settlement patterns within notionally bounded areas, such as parishes, often reflected a relationship with woodlands. The classic Medieval model of a nucleated settlement, for example on the claylands of the Midlands, might be at the centre of an open field system with woodlands on the periphery, although within an accessible distance. John Steane notes (1984:159) that 'many villages were 6.4 km from any wood and many others were a day's journey from a substantial piece of woodland'.

The systems of trackways and settlements associated with the Anglo-Saxon use of the landscape of England also included extensive and substantial banking (Hoskins, 1955). These banks might define ownership of estates and blocks of resources, such as fields and woods. That banking rather than, for example, hawthorn hedging, was selected as the means of dividing land suggests a statement of ownership and control rather than mere practicality. It implies a permanent re-ordering of the landscape using a different set of concepts, seeking perhaps to eradicate earlier claims to ownership.

The extent of woodlands in England as a whole, as represented in the Domesday Book survey of AD1086, is difficult to gauge, and will be discussed below in more detail, with specific reference to the North Downs and Cudham. Oliver Rackham estimates that of the 27 million acres of England covered by the survey, only 15%, or 4.1 million acres were woodland, with an uneven geographical distribution (1995a:51). The subsequent decline in the amount of woodland over the following 800 years occurred principally, he argues, in well-wooded counties.

The woodlands of the Early and Late Medieval periods took a variety of forms, with complex management regimes (discussed by Peterken, 1993). Coppice would be cut on a rotational cycle that varied between 6 and 15 years, dependent on the growth rate of individual species, demand for coppice products and the labour available to carry out the harvest. Cropping would rarely include complete clearance of a woodland area. A field layer would be left under the mature woodland for use as stock grazing, given that the animals would be unable to reach the higher growth, whilst they would eradicate new shoots in freshly cropped areas of the wood. This system implies permanent subdivisions within the coppice woodlands, in the form of hedges and banks. Invasive species, such as birch, would need to be controlled as they would inhibit re-growth of the coppice stools. Generally, the species that were cropped were native to the wood and were not specifically planted. Standards within the coppice were generally felled when small, with a basal diameter of approximately 45cm (Peterken, 1993:22). The timing of this crop might coincide with a multiple of the coppice cycle. Young standards might be protected from animal grazing by a ring of thorn bushes. Standards were also commonly present in hedgerows.

Perhaps the most common form of woodland in the Medieval period was wood pasture. This contained a combination of tree forms, together with herbage for grazing. As a management practice it may have originated in prehistory from the pasturing of cattle in the wildwood (Peterken, 1993:12). In order to avoid over-grazing causing damage to the trees, and to avoid the trees over-shadowing and thus reducing the amount of grazing, a balanced system was produced. This might involve a low density of standards, or alternatively the use of pollarding, the practice of coppicing trees above the level of human and animal reach. Pollarding prolongs the life of the tree, with this most enduring tree form often associated with the marking of estate and parish boundaries. Wood pasture was the most likely form of the common woods, parks and forests of the Medieval period. Other woodland grazing areas were provided by rides and launds, that is, permanent clearings within and through the woodlands.

Woodlands were a form of wealth in the later Medieval period (AD900-1550). Landowners could use them to supply the needs of their manorial estates and sell off the surplus in the burgeoning market economy of the period. Although stone and brick buildings became more common from the thirteenth and fourteenth centuries (Clarke, 1984:37), timber remained the principal building material in both urban and rural settlements. Framing material for rural peasant houses of the fifteenth century appears to have been purchased, rather than taken from owned sources (Dyer, 1986:28). As fuel, in the form of charcoal, underwood, or coppice material, woodland products had a major importance as a resource for both domestic and industrial uses, for example in the Medieval Wealden iron industry (discussed by Bolton,1980:192-3).

In theory, all land in the later Medieval period belonged to the crown and was held by individuals in return for services and rents, in a complex system of obligations and rights. Common rights to wood pasture and wooded wasteland, many established in the Early Medieval period (AD450-900), controlled and restricted access to a fluctuating resource. Areas such as Andred's Weald covering parts of Kent, Surrey and Sussex, and Sherwood (Shirewood) Forest in Nottinghamshire were available as common woods for their county (Peterken, 1993:13). Customary *botes* were the rights of individuals to cut wood from the lord of the manor's estate for specific purposes, such the right of *estover*, to cut fuel or fencing. However, not all manors contained woodland within their own boundaries and they may have had rights to woods in other, more distant areas. For example, the manor of Bignor, West Sussex, had an outlier wood at Kirdford, five miles away in the Weald (Gardiner,1984:75). Large tracts of wooded and scrubland areas were enclosed from the eleventh century onwards, either as private manorial deer parks or as substantial royal forests for hunting, for example the New Forest in Hampshire. Indeed, the whole county of Surrey was declared forest in the twelfth century (VCH Surrey, 1905:561). The areas that were enclosed often included commons, which themselves rarely survived as intact entities into the post-Medieval period. The process of assarting, or the piecemeal clearing and enclosure of land, including commons, heaths and moors, initially for arable and later for grazing, diminished the woodlands further in the twelfth and thirteenth centuries (Hoskins, 1955:87), particularly as new settlements were established. Williamson and Bellamy note (1987:83) that within woodland areas 'this produced a pattern of scattered farmsteads, most of which proclaimed the newly-won status of their owners by being endowed with moats'. The continuing depletion of standing timber for building purposes prompted attempts at the conservation of resources (Stamper,1983). The importation of straight grained timber into England from the south east Baltic, via the merchants of the Hanseatic League, is evident from the fifteenth century.

Peterken suggests the use of the terms 'Ancient' woodland and post-Medieval or 'Recent' woodland to distinguish between those with origins before and after a threshold date of AD1600. Hoskins (1955:137) gives statistics for the late seventeenth century which estimate the presence of three million acres of woods and coppices, and another three million acres of forests, parks and commons. This represents a significant decrease in the overall extent of woodland since the beginning of that century. Woodland as a capital resource is evidenced in this period by the auction of the Forest of Dean to realise income for the crown in the 1630s, resulting in the clear felling of one-third of its total acreage within a year (Schama, 1995:158).

In the post-Medieval period large areas of remaining British woodlands were grubbed out to provide arable and grazing, most markedly in the Agricultural Revolution of the eighteenth century (Darby, 1951:81). Whilst a few small freeholders in the woodland areas survived against this background of enclosure, much of the landscape became dominated by large estates, owned by the aristocracy and the landed gentry. There was, however, also a simultaneous trend towards afforestation through new plantations, often with non-native species, many of them conifers. The creation of particular habitats, such as fox coverts and ornamental parklands, reflected changing attitudes to the landscape engendered by the ideas of the Enlightenment (Daniels, 1988). These ideas suggested that 'it was now possible to re-arrange the landscape to suit the owner's taste' (Gold, 1984:22). As a result, many earlier forms of land-use became partially erased from the landscape, although the remains of woodland banking could still be discerned as linear earthworks running through parks, grassland and arable fields.

Peterken (1993:22) notes a period of coppice improvement from the seventeenth century onwards. In the south-east of England, hazel and chestnut were planted as underwood, within a more systematically laid out, regularly compartmentalised regime that included marginal ditches and wide rides. Small, secondary woodlands, or copses, were newly created in the enclosed landscape, with oak, ash and beech the dominant species. Boys (1796:121) describes the woodland industry of east Kent, where the woods were mainly situated on the flint with clay soils, thus indicating a re-wooding of the Downs in that era.

He comments that the slow growth of trees on chalk soils produced timber of little value. The main product was hop-poles from trees on the hill tops, with chestnut, ash, willow and maple producing the best sort, whilst beech and hornbeam produced inferior poles. Beech and hornbeam standards were used for the piles in sea walls, whilst oak and birch provided pit props for coal mines in Newcastle. The woodlands of Kent increased from 85,000 acres, in 1888, to 98,000 acres by 1905, of which 75,000 acres were coppice (Victoria County History of Kent, 1908, vol.1:474).

The net decline of woodlands in the British Isles has been reversed in the twentieth century, with a doubling of the wooded area in the last eighty years (Peterken, 1993:85). This has been almost exclusively in the form of mono-cultures of conifers. In lowland areas planting has occurred on less productive ground, such as the East Anglian heaths, in small, scattered stands. Whilst it might be argued that the afforestation is replacing woodland in areas that were covered in wildwood in an earlier period, concurrent with this process is a decreasing range of ground flora and habitat for fauna that is demonstrably different from that of the wildwood.

The woodlands of the British Isles have therefore changed considerably over time. In a given area, such as a county, the woodlands might have had different forms, might vary in density and are not necessarily always in the same place. The erosion of the woodlands has not been an even process, as changing cultural imperatives, such as the growing market economy of the later Medieval period, have impacted differently in different places. Areas of ancient woodland have, though, survived to attest to this changing culture of woodland use, although commonly in fragmented forms. Peterken indicates (1993:40) that the most intensive concentrations of ancient woodland occur in the south east of England, around the Chilterns, the New Forest, the Weald and on the North Downs.

WOODLANDS STUDIES: A LITERATURE REVIEW

Archaeological and historical studies of settlement and land use patterns within woodlands have sought to draw out both the details of change within the Medieval period and the underlying cultural processes that were fundamental to those changes. These studies have taken place on both the small scale of parishes and on the larger scale of regions.

Tom Williamson (1988:5-13) discusses the 'woodland' landscapes of the Early Medieval period. Within the south and east of England they formed a continuous belt surrounding the London Basin, defined to the west by the line of the Chiltern escarpment and included the counties to the east on either side of the Thames estuary. In 'woodland' areas the field systems were irregular and associated with 'a dispersed pattern of settlement ... characterised by a profusion of ... hamlets or isolated farms' (1988:5). He suggests that this pattern had its roots in 'definable social and economic processes' (1988:6), for example the custom of partible inheritance in Anglo-Saxon society, whereby the land holding was divided amongst heirs rather given to a sole inheritor. Whilst dispersed settlement and irregular field systems have been associated with the later Medieval process of assarting, primarily the enclosure of marginal lands on poor soils, in contrast in the south east of England this pattern occurs on all soil types. Indeed, Williamson suggests that assarting in general did not inevitably lead to settlement dispersal. If population pressure, Williamson argues (1988:7), has been cited as a possible cause of village nucleation and the advent of large open fields elsewhere in England, for example on the claylands of the Midlands in the century and a half before AD1086, then the south east of England would appear to have been under populated in this period, by virtue of its non-nucleation. Analysis of the Domesday Book entries based on population and plough team densities suggests that this was not the case, and reference must be again made here to the exceptionally high number of plough teams (ten) cited for Cudham. The causes of the continuation of a dispersed settlement pattern in the woodlands of south east England are therefore varied, perhaps the result of a combination of factors, such as a 'discrete pattern of land holding ... combined with ... the poorly developed nature of communal systems of organisation (which) allowed a greater fluidity of settlement' (Williamson, 1988:9).

The greater density of woodland in the south east in the Medieval period, in comparison to the Midland areas, may have inhibited the process of settlement nucleation. A pattern of settlement dispersal within the woodlands can be demonstrated to have continued in the south east throughout the Medieval and post-Medieval periods, indicating that factors other than population expansion and land hunger were solely responsible for its continuation. Whatever these further causes, Williamson sees the roots of the pattern in the 'importance of extended kindreds as a prime force in land-holding and resource allocation' that were slower to decline in the south east in comparison to the Midlands (1988:12). The concentration of place-names in woodland areas with the element *ingas*, meaning 'people of', perhaps indicates 'the land-holding of an extended kindred', indicating territorial rather than specific place settlement (1988:12). On the Downs and the dip-slope, in the vicinity of Cudham, attention is drawn to the place-names Warlingham, Woldingham, Addington (all in Surrey), Orpington and Kemsing (in Kent).

Della Hooke (1989:113-129) discusses the usage of woodlands in the West Midlands during the Anglo-Saxon period. She suggests that hunting, and the organisation of the woodlands as game reserves, was a widespread phenomenon that was important before the eleventh century. Indeed, rather than being solely a Norman innovation, this form of land use was known in the Frankish kingdoms of north west Europe from the seventh century (1989:129), and she cites charter evidence for Kemsing noting hunting rights dated to AD822 (1989:122). Importantly for this discussion of woodlands in Cudham, which was situated on the western edge of the early Anglo-Saxon kingdom of Kent, she discusses the place-name term *haga* which occurs 'most frequently in more remote, less-developed regions where thick woodland was plentiful' (1989:123). She suggests that, in Germany, *haga* place-names are associated with 'fortified settlements established along province frontiers', but that they were a development of the enclosure of woodland to contain wild animals. In England, the term related to defended settlements, which she suggests may have been linked to royal ownership (1989:123). A case is made for a linguistic relationship between *haga* and the Middle English term *hay*, most commonly evident within place-names as *hayes*, 'a small hunting park, usually in a woodland area, enclosed for the retention of deer' (1989:125). It is noted that Hayes Common lies in the parish of Keston, adjacent to Cudham, on the dip-slope of the Downs.

Substantial lengths of banks and ditches are associated with some *haga* enclosures in the West Midlands. Although difficult to distinguish from other banking in the landscape, for example those to enclose deer parks, their form is suggested as being a wide bank and ditch, surmounted by a timber palisade or a substantial hedge (Hooke, 1989:128). The word *haga* is also connected with haw, found in hawthorn, suggesting a thorn hedge. The area of land enclosed in this manner varied, with some relatively short lengths of banking and others which extended for many kilometres '…sometimes appearing to enclose almost entire estates' (1989:123).

Whilst there are no studies focusing specifically on the woodlands of the North Downs, Roden's study of *Woodland and its management in the Medieval Chilterns* (1968) does provide comparative material from a chalk upland environment similar to that of Cudham. Documentary sources on which the study is based indicate that '…many woods were worked for profit as early as the thirteenth century' (1968:60). This coincided with an end to clearing for agriculture, despite the pressure of population increase in the period, as the value of woodland resources began to outstrip that for arable. Assarting had ended by AD1300, leaving '…a pattern of woodland that remained basically unchanged for 300 years' (1968:59) and included both private and common woodland. These woodlands had different forms of tree management, which reflected their differing economic roles.

Private woodlands occurred not only as part of the manorial demesne or park, but also as large subdivided woods, reflecting the enclosure of woods by different people. These woods might have internal divisions marked by fences or ditches. Roden comments that '…by the second half of the twelfth century plots of timber were being freely granted, sold and leased in the same way as arable or meadow ..... Consolidation counterbalanced fragmentation, and, together with the active market in wooded parcels, was a further indication of the value of woodland' (1968:63).

In addition, there were small groves of trees, attached to settlements or situated between fields. Roden notes the term 'cultivated groves' as an …'intermixture of cultivated land and wood in a single enclosed unit' (1968:64) that occurred on the sides of valleys in the Chiltern Hills. The systems of management are unclear, but the documentary sources imply selective felling of standards for the funding and resourcing of capital projects, such as public and private buildings. Roden suggests (1968:64) that the main cause of the creation and survival of private woodland, even on good agricultural soil, was the supply of underwood products, particularly for fuel, sent down the river Thames to London.

CUDHAM

Common woodlands, particularly if lying in more than one parish, might be used as a resource by a number of settlements and households. More open in character than private woods, they had little underwood with larger areas for grazing. With the felling of the standards, they tended to degenerate into open scrub and semi heath, as had occurred to many of them by the seventeenth century.

Roden notes (1968:67) that in the post-Medieval period there was a substantial reduction in the wooded areas of the Chilterns, with the better soils turned over to arable farming. The remaining woodland was concentrated on the poorer soils and on the steeper slopes, a pattern which was reinforced by the location of plantations in the eighteenth century. As a result, some woodlands now exist on what had been farmland in the seventeenth century.

Witney (1990) considers the woodland economy of Kent as a whole in the period AD1066-1348, that is, between the appropriation by Norman landlords of Anglo-Saxon land holdings and the depopulation and economic decline associated with the Black Death. He describes a situation, in the mid to late eleventh century, of a county with abundant woodland. In the Early Medieval period, once the Jutes from north-west Europe re-settled Roman land holdings in east Kent and expanded onto the adjacent better soils in the fifth and sixth centuries, it is probable that the wooded areas, and the Downs in particular, were under exploited and not systematically managed. Settlement on the Downs was mainly achieved through small scale clearances, although Witney (1990:36) also notes, without explanation, the exceptional number of ploughs associated with Cudham. Seasonal transhumance, whereby pigs from manors north of the Downs, such as Lewisham and Bromley, were driven in large numbers to the dens of the Weald in order to be fattened up by feeding on fallen acorns, declined rapidly throughout this period. Witney suggests that these northerly manors rather made use of the Downs landscape, accessed via the existing transhumance track-ways, for the intermittent pasturing of draught stock, probably oxen. The evidence of place-names occurring on the Downs that include the elements *steall*, *stoc* and *sol*, the latter meaning shallow pond, support this view (1990:26).

The changes that occurred in the nature of Kentish woodlands in the two centuries following the Norman Conquest were caused primarily by population growth and the demands of the expanding network of towns. These factors led both to land hunger and to a demand for more arable production to support the urban population. The need for wood fuel in the towns and fencing for fields and deer parks meant that systematic management was a necessity, predominantly a system of coppice with standards. By the thirteenth century '...the value of woods had risen far beyond that of any other type of land' (Witney, 1990:33).

Sections of the Weald were cleared for new settlement, mainly those that were too far distant from the main transport routes that might have facilitated the economic sale of woodland products. The pressure of land hunger within older settled communities was thus relieved. In contrast, for manors and places already settled, such as Eltham and Bexley north of the Downs, it was worthwhile to use land to cultivate woodland products for London. The tension between clearance and the management of woodlands, between illicit felling and assarting and the lords' investment policies for profit, is illustrated in numerous court cases of the time (discussed by Witney, 1990:37). The tension ceased, however, with the depredations and depopulation caused by the Black Death which '...knocked the bottom out of the wood market' (1990:37). Given the poor soils of the Downs woodlands and the reduction in demand for new land, it was no longer economic to clear them for timber or for conversion to arable farming. The existing pattern of woodland was further fixed on the landscape 'as the population began to pick up (and) such innovations as hop-growing gave a renewed value to the coppices on the Downs and elsewhere' (Witney, 1990:39).

That the system of land use in the areas surrounding the Thames Basin was strongly influenced by the dominant needs of London at its core is further evidenced by Campbell et al's 1992 study *Rural Land-use in the Metropolitan Hinterland, 1270-1339: the Evidence of Inquisitiones Post Mortem*. These assessments, or IPMs, carried out on the death of the tenant in chief of the crown, detailed, to varying degrees, the value and types of land on the demesne of individual manors. They highlight the complex and changing nature of manorial holdings in the later Medieval period. The period covered by this particular study was one of looming agrarian crisis, wherein the growing population of London (estimated at between 80-100 thousand in AD1300 most of whom were engaged in non-agricultural activities) was impacting on the resource base of the hinterland. Whilst not dealing explicitly with woodlands, the authors of this study do note a relationship between the large size of the arable holding of a demesne and the incidence of a park. In Essex, for example, demesnes in excess of 300 acres of arable with associated parks are evident. Cudham, with an average amount of arable on the demesne of between 75 and 150 acres, also has a park, in contrast to other manors of comparable size which generally did not (Campbell et al, 1992:12-13). Apart from those in the vicinity of the River Thames, no parks other than Cudham's are noted from IPMs for the whole of the West Kent area (1992:12, fig.3).

From their examination of the values of demesne resources, and therefore not including common lands, Campbell et al conclude (1992: 21) that 'London lay in the midst of a predominantly arable-farming region, but not one that was characterised by uniform soils and terrain, nor by a uniform institutional structure.....it seems likely that the capital influenced its hinterland in terms of the impact, which its demands for necessities had upon the emergence of specialised agrarian regimes'.

There is evidence to support a view that woodlands constituted a specialised regime of production on the periphery of London's hinterland in the Later Medieval period. Paul Stamper (1983) discusses the documentary evidence for the Medieval royal forest of Pamber in Hampshire. He concludes that it formed a resource that was used for royal patronage, even though small in area. Timber from there, that is, the product of felled standards, was transported widely '...across central southern England' (1983:51), until a change in royal policy, away from one of conservation management to clear felling without replacement, led to a substantial overall reduction in its area. By the thirteenth century, this land had been released for assarting.

In the context of the agricultural regimes of the North Downs, Mary Saaler (1996) discusses the fourteenth century manorial accounts of the manor of Farleigh, near to Cudham but on the Surrey side of the county boundary (see location map, fig.1). This was a relatively small manor of 1051 acres, exhibiting a mixed agricultural system. Arable crops and pasture accounted for two thirds of the acreage, but woodland products for fuel and timber for building were also consistently present. She comments that '...the accounts mentioned specific areas of woodland which were cropped for firewood, notably the west wood, le Frith (now Frith Wood) and the park' (1996:61). Sales of bundles of faggots fell significantly after the Black Death. Timber was mainly used for building work on the manor or was converted into roof shingles and laths. Additional products included hurdles for the sheep fold and 100 dung baskets, as noted in AD1356. Bark was a by-product that was used in tanning processes, reference to which is noted in the Court Roll for AD1329. An enquiry of AD1364 adjudicated on the illicit sale of 400 timber trees to people outside the manor. She concludes that '…this evidence suggests that woodland products were being moved within a radius of about 24km from Farleigh', (1996:61), indicating that the distance from there to London for bulky materials was not insurmountable.

From this, albeit selective, literature review of recent studies of woodland settlement and land use in the Medieval period, a dominant factor has emerged. The woodland periphery of the London Basin, characterised by its dispersed settlement pattern, came under stress during the economic pressures of the thirteenth and fourteenth centuries, due mainly to the economic, social and recreational demands of the growing urban centre in London. The people of Cudham could have responded by developing a vigorous economy based on the sale of woodland products. Due to the non-intensive labour needs of such a form of production and because of the probable relatively low density of population, the potential for profitability was certainly present. Whether such a potential was exploited and whether it can provide an explanation for the distribution of Cudham's woodlands remains to be examined further. The extent to which this may indeed have been the case encounters the anomaly of a Downland landscape that may have been dominated by a park, itself perhaps dating from the earliest Anglo-Saxon use of the North Downs.

THE ENVIRONMENT AND GEOLOGY OF CUDHAM PARISH

The parish of Cudham lies wholly on the north facing slopes of the North Downs. Its lowest point on its northern boundary (TQ456633) is 85m above sea level, but over its 7km length it rises to a high point of 243m (TQ435566). Here it overlooks the chalk scarp of the Downs to the south, and occupies the highest point along the whole length of these hills. The southernmost part, designated an Area of Outstanding Natural Beauty, might be characterised as an upland, with a noticeably different climate to that of the lower areas at Bromley and Orpington, that is, colder and wetter with a later spring. The Cudham section of the North Downs constitutes the wettest part of the Greater London area, with Biggin Hill recorded as attracting an average 800mm (32") of rainfall per annum.

The Downs consist of chalk, with cappings of clay with flints. Throughout their north-south axis runs a network of steep-sided, thin soiled, dry valleys, exposing areas of the upper and middle chalk, with deeper alluvial deposits along their length (see fig.4). The Downs around Biggin Hill on the western part of the parish form the headwaters of the River Ravensbourne, which rises at Keston, further north down the slope. The eastern slopes of the parish constitute the headwaters of the River Cray, which rises at Orpington. These watercourses eventually feed into the River Thames at Deptford and Crayford respectively. The surface geology shows an open clay plateau divided into rounded hills by the intercutting valleys. There are no streams currently flowing off the Downs through Cudham, however. The high level of seasonal run-off of water has recently necessitated the construction of a drainage lake in the Biggin Hill valley, in a field named the Lord's Croft (TQ411599). On the plateaux above the valleys are intermittent, flint-lined dew ponds, associated with the current farmsteads. Burton comments '… clay does not allow water to pass through it and drainage can only be by surface run-off, so the extent to which the soil becomes waterlogged will vary according to whether the ground is level, with little scope for movement of water through the soil, or sloping … (although) steeply sloping clay surfaces are notoriously subject to slipping …' (1983:ix). Additionally it is remarked that '…horse drawn ploughs could get farther up the field than modern machines' (1983:xiv). It is further noted that cereal crops are unable to form adequate roots in clay and that most of the Ancient woodlands in the Greater London area are sited on London clay, with hawthorn an abundant species therein.

The current land use within the parish, apart from the airport at Biggin Hill and the associated urban developments, is mainly agricultural '…with pasture predominant on the plateau and arable land concentrated in the valley bottoms' (Hayes, 1995:7). The small, irregularly shaped woodlands are mainly concentrated on the valley sides, some of which are secondary woods, the result of an intermittent abandonment of grazing (see woodlands map, fig.2). The borough of Bromley contains 32% of the remaining Ancient woodland in the Greater London area, with the greatest density of these occurring in Cudham. The largest single wood is Cudham Frith, although this suffered severe internal damage as a result of the Great Storm of October 1987. The Downland woods were systematically harvested during the Second World War. Alister Hayes comments 'Several woodlands show a coppice with standards structure. This comprises a coppice tree species such as hazel, ash or beech under standards of oak, beech or maple. Many of these woodlands have become derelict following the cessation of active management in the early part of the century, whilst others show changes in management practice with coniferous species being planted amongst the coppice. Following the woodland clearance of the last few centuries, thin strips of woodland remain, known as shaws' (1994:19). Also present within the parish

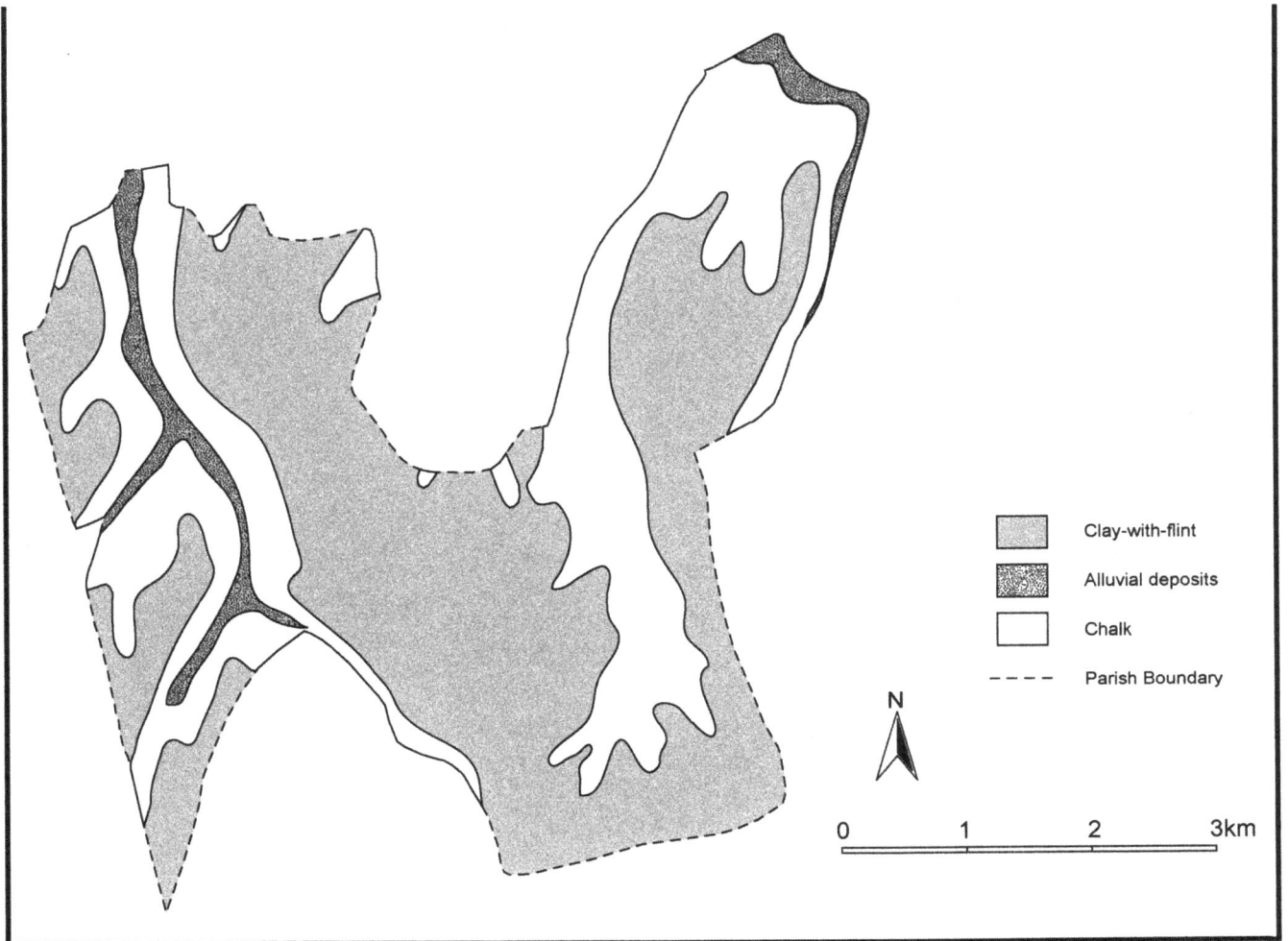

FIGURE 4. GEOLOGICAL MAP OF CUDHAM

are hedgerows, framing the rights of way and delineating fields, and pollarded trees, which are situated on the parish and estate boundaries.

THE DOCUMENTARY EVIDENCE FOR CUDHAM

The parish of Cudham as an entity has not been the subject of extended historical research. Whilst primary sources for the manors of Cudham do exist, the following discussion is based on secondary, mainly antiquarian generated, sources. The documentary references do not reflect directly on the woodlands that are the principal concern of this research. The documents can provide, however, an insight into the economic and social changes that took place in Cudham in the later Medieval and post-Medieval periods.

The earliest known reference to Cudham comes from the *Textus Roffensis*, a record of the diocese of Rochester dating from AD982 (discussed by Pearman, n.d.). This document notes the payment of 7d for chrysm oil, indicating the existence of a properly consecrated church in Cudham that was carrying out baptism.

The Domesday Book of AD1086 was drawn up as an inventory of land and property values, in order to take stock of the revenue accruing to the crown in the period after the Norman Conquest of AD1066. It is an incomplete survey of England, although meticulous in the regions that it does cover. There are regional variations, reflecting a diversity of local customs in the methods of taxation. Although the data is limited in some respects, notably in regard to the extent of woodland in this period, it is possible to reconstruct aspects of the rural economy of the places named in the text.

Oliver Rackham asserts (1995b:75) that only approximately 50% of places in AD1086 possessed woodland, with, for example, those within a thirty-five mile radius of London each having a wood, whilst there was none at all in areas such as the Fens. Large tracts of woodland were still extant, such as in the Weald, at Blean in Kent and on the Chiltern plateau. In Kent, Witney suggests that the Downs …'were thickly scattered with woods along their entire length and carried certain larger areas of forest ….The woods.... contained some oak but as much beech and hornbeam, together with a variety of trees, yew, whitebeam, maple and alder, of less economic value' (1990:21). Alan Everitt (1986:155) has identified a continuous line of forest from Luxted, in the parish of Downe adjacent to Cudham, to Joydens Wood 13 kilometres away to the north east. In addition, the poor soils to the north of the Downs around Hayes and Chislehurst were also left as woodland. Arable farming was concentrated on the richer soils on either side of the Downs. Judging by the distribution of Domesday Book place-names (Campbell, 1962:501), the western Kentish section of the North Downs was sparsely settled, with Cudham's nearest named neighbour, Otford, 8km to the east. The system of landholding on the Downs in the pre-Conquest period was markedly different to that of the Original Lands, or areas of earliest known settlement on the richer soils (Everitt, 1986:176). The formative influences on the fragmented settlement pattern evident on the Downs are suggested by Everitt as comprising the uninviting nature of the terrain in comparison to the corn-growing areas; the seasonal pastoral use of the Downs which had eventually led to more permanent use of the summer shielings; the distance from the centralised control exercised by estate centres on the Original Lands, leading to a the evolution of an independent society on the frontier of land colonisation; the tenurial system of gavelkind whereby freemen paid rent for land and had a relatively small amount of labour service due to the lord, and finally the system of partible inheritance. Everitt characterises this pre-Conquest environment on the Downs as an 'old and deeply-rooted local world' (1986:177).

It is within this context that the Domesday Book entry for Cudham must be considered, and it is immediately apparent that this entry is unusual in many respects. This assertion is most readily examined by considering the text in detail. The full translation of the entry is as follows:

Gilbert Maminot holds of the bishop Codeham. It is assessed at 4 sulungs. There is land for 10 ploughs. On the demesne are 4, and 15 villeins with 6 bordars have 6 ploughs. A church is there, and 11 serfs and 2 mills worth 14 shillings and 2 pence, and woodland (to render) 40 swine. T.R.E. it was worth 20 pounds, afterwards 16 pounds, now 24 pounds (Victoria County History: Kent, 1908, vol.3:224).

The bishop was Odo of Bayeux, brother of King William. Gilbert Maminot was one of his tenants. This entry marks the removal of the manor from Anglo-Saxon ownership. Cudham was part of a tranche of 62 estates on the North Downs (out of a total of 93 on the Downs listed in the Domesday Book) given to the bishop, making him by far the biggest landowner on the Downs in this period. In contrast to the Original Lands of settlement, where ownership continued to be dominated by the church, the Downs represented a swathe of land that was predominantly in private, independent ownership, and perhaps more susceptible to re-allocation. The crown had no holdings on the Downs, although the church, through, for example, the Archbishop of Canterbury, held the majority of the remaining manors (Everitt, 1986:173).

The assessment of sulungs indicates the number of units of taxation that might be levied against the manor. A sulung is a term peculiar to Kent, and is estimated as being the equivalent of between 180 and 200 acres (Campbell, 1962:503), that is, an area that could be worked by a plough team of eight oxen (Whitelock, 1965:68). Thus, Cudham might have 800 acres of arable land that would support the payment of tax. This land would, however, also include meadow, pasture and woodland and is described as 'privileged freeholds of which the occupiers were primarily rent payers owing very little in the way of labour services' (Witney,1987:108). Sulungs are perhaps related to land seizures by the new settlers of the early Anglo-Saxon period, and their distribution marks the pattern of that settlement. In some Domesday Book entries two assessments are given. Bromley was assessed at six sulungs before 1066, but only three in 1086. As a remission in tax assessment, this might indicate favouritism by the crown, given that the bishop held Bromley directly, or perhaps a perceived loss of value due to upheavals resulting from the Norman invasion. The assessment for Cudham remained at four sulungs. When compared to those manors in Kent to the north and west of Cudham, only Bromley had a higher assessment, with most other manors in the locality assessed at between a half and two sulungs . The manor of Otford in the Darenth valley, held by the Archbishop, was assessed at eight sulungs. Manors over the border in Surrey were assessed for hides, each one being approximately equivalent to half a sulung (Witney,1990:109), and was 'originally the amount of land felt sufficient for a peasant household' (Whitelock,1965:68). All the Surrey manors near to Cudham were substantially reassessed down by AD1086, although Chelsham, the manor adjacent to Cudham on the top of the Downs, had been liable for the not inconsiderable 10 hides, Addington for eight and Farleigh for six. As a group of settlements on the Downs, these manors were at least as valuable as those on lower lying areas. Indeed, the value of Cudham, as recorded in the Domesday assessment, actually increased in the eleventh century. Thus, Cudham appears economically to have been relatively unaffected by the political and social changes occurring elsewhere.

There was no direct correspondence, however, between the tax assessment, based on an earlier system of land use, and the agricultural resources of a manor in AD1086, which is dealt with in the next part of the entry, relating to ploughlands. A ploughland might be surmised as representing 100 acres (Brandon and Short, 1990:36), giving an approximate equivalence for Cudham to the earlier sulung based assessment of between 800-1000 acres. The number of ploughlands and their relationship to the number of plough teams in a manor varies with each Domesday Book entry. Campbell (1962:508) notes a deficiency of teams against ploughlands in one-third of the entries for Kent, perhaps indicating under-population and lack of resources on a local scale. Another third of the entries exhibit an increase in the number of plough teams against the land available, thus indicating pressure on the resource base within a restricted area. Cudham, however, shows a constant and exact relationship over time between plough teams and land for ploughing.

The demesne, or land held by the lord as his own estate and on which labour dues were worked, contains, in the case of Cudham, a higher proportion of plough teams than is found elsewhere. For example, in Bromley there were only two ploughs in lordship, in comparison to Cudham's four in lordship, but 11ploughs were worked by the villagers there, in contrast to the six in Cudham (Crozier and Philp, 1985:14). Commonly, in this area of the Downs and its dip slope, the lord held only one or two ploughs.

The structure of Cudham society at the time of the Domesday Book assessment is also discernible. Reference to 15 villeins and six bordars probably indicates the number of households of freemen and labourers, probably representing a population of 100 people. The 11 serfs, or slaves, might refer to individuals rather than to households. The number of serfs was perhaps higher as a proportion of population than was common amongst the lower lying manors. The density of population in Cudham and their number of associated ploughteams was not actually above average for the period however, although it might appear so from the documentary source. If the abnormally large size of the manor at 5925 acres is brought into consideration (based on the modern parish size), together with the dispersed settlement pattern, the population density and the numbers of ploughs that these people worked was comparable to that of neighbouring manors. Unfortunately, it has been common practice to compare Cudham to Kentish manors, where it does stand out as having a large number of ploughs, rather than to others also on the Downs in Surrey. Titsey, to the south and west of Cudham, had 54 units of population with 13 ploughs, whilst Chelsham, the neighbouring manor to the west covering 3357 acres, had 42 units of population with 11 ploughs.

Settlements in Kent, according to the Domesday Book entries for the county, commonly had only one mill, usually sited on and driven by a stream or river. The Cudham entry stands out here, as it was the only manor on land above 125m to have any mills at all recorded against its name (Campbell, 1962:542). Whilst each mill in Cudham was not exceptionally valuable, the possession of two mills does give an indication of the scale of arable production. Problematically, wind powered mill technology was an innovation of the late twelfth century (Steane, 1984:170). This therefore suggests that the Cudham mills may have been driven by animal or human power, given the absence of watercourses on the Downs. Alternatively, the mills may have been sited elsewhere outside of the manor, possibly linked to the later attested ownership of the manor at Marsh Green in Holmesdale, situated on a tributary of the river Eden.

The 'swine render' relates to the annual rent paid by the local people to the lord for the right to pannage their pigs in his wood. It is an estimate of expected income, based on the woodland resources available. The 40 pigs in the Cudham swine render represent 10% of the total stock owned by the local population. It is problematic to convert this number of pigs into an estimate of the amount of woodland within a manor, as there would also have been common woods available for pannage and the entry may also relate to rights over woods in other places. The manor of Orpington to the north east of Cudham in the Upper Cray Valley had, for example, five pig pastures of woodland for the render of 50 pigs. This may have been in conflict with the 25 ploughs within this parish of 3517 acres, and suggests that these pig pastures may indeed have been sited elsewhere, with nearby Cudham a prime candidate for their location. In general, the Domesday Book makes little explicit reference to woods. They must therefore be assumed to have been ubiquitous, as a shortage of supply might increase the amount of revenue that could be accrued from them, and thus be worthy of note. Cudham appears to have rendered considerably more pigs than many surrounding manors, with only the woodlands of Bromley and Beckenham rendering more. The implication of the entry for swine renders is the presence of significant areas of oak trees, although this may not necessarily have been the dominant tree species on the Downs in this period.

From this discussion of the Domesday Book entry for Cudham several aspects of its landscape and economy have emerged. The initial impression of a place dominated economically by arable farming is supported, particularly as mills are cited as being present. It also appears as a remote place, relatively untouched by the political upheavals of the eleventh century, retaining its prosperity and its long settled way of life. The exceptionally large size of the parish, at nearly 6000 acres, counteracts the impression of a densely populated and intensively worked landscape. Indeed, the comparisons discussed above indicate that, if anything, it was under populated and under exploited. Although the woodlands are not explicit in the entry, it might be characterised as a place surrounded by and existing within the woodlands that had not been completely cleared since the earliest settlement of the Downs.

Steinman (1851:3) suggests that the parish of Cudham, in the later Medieval period, was the location for three manors. The manor of Cudham is recorded in the thirteenth century by a short series of Inquisitions Post Mortem (IPM), or assessments of the extent of the land and value of a manor, carried out at the time of the death of the owner. The IPM for AD1269 links Cudham with a tranche of property in Halstead and Godington, these being settlements lying to the east, and makes particular reference to gavelkind land. The IPM for AD1295 notes rents due to the manor of 10 plough shares worth 8d each, possibly signifying a consistency with the Domesday record, and a cart and a half worth 3s a cart, probably referring to loads of underwood or coppice products. Unfortunately, the full extent of the manor, although recorded in IPMs, is not published for these entries. Fortunately, Steinman (1851:3) recorded in full the IPM for AD1272, extracts from which are cited below:

... in the said manor 200 acres of arable land ... at 2d per acre ... 104 acres of waste land at 1d each acre ... there are at Betrede, which belongs to the said manor, 164 acres of arable land at 2d each acre. Of meadow nothing ... in the park of Codham and the wood of Bokehurst 100 acres of pasture at 3d each acre ... there are in the park of Betrede 30 acres and the pasture is worth in the said park ... 4d each acre. Item there are there 200 acres of wood, of which there are there of underwood 150 acres, which may be sold, and which is worth ... 12d each acre ... the pannage in the said wood is worth 12s when it happens ... of rents of assize of the free tenants of Codham and Bertred £17 per annum ... of rents of assize of 14 ploughshares ... at 8d each ploughshare. The sum of the extent of this manor £33 4s 4d.

This assessment highlights a situation in the thirteenth century wherein the most valuable form of land use was woodland pasture, and that the rents paid by the free tenantry made up more than half of the manorial income. The woodland pasture of the parks had, therefore, a greater monetary value than the arable. The sale of coppice products, whilst relatively valuable, only provided an intermittent income, dependent on the periodicity of the coppicing cycle. Labour services on the demesne were discounted as not being worth the trouble to demand.

In AD1322 the Kent Feet of Fines noted that the manor of Cudham included pasture in the parks of Cudham and Bertre, and in Frithe and Bocherst. By AD1360 a further record noted land belonging to the manor in Bederede, Northberden, Suthberden, Thornefeld and Mede, together with a park for deer, for the keeping of which the parker was paid 14d per week.

Hasted (1801:62) notes the granting of the right of free-warren on the demesne in AD1335. The term free-warren refers to the exclusive right to hunt, and relates to both the types of creature, such as fox, badger or deer, that could be hunted and to the place where this right might be exercised (Cantor, 1982:82). This was a common manorial right in the fourteenth century. The manor of Cudham also had ownership of the manor of Marsh Green in the Weald, near Edenbridge (Victoria County History of Kent).

The manor of Apuldrefield appears to be a post-Conquest creation, with the earliest reference to the name appearing in AD1191, when it was held as a knight's fee from the manor of Cudham. It comprised a parcel of lands, with the demesne estate estimated at 496 acres. This was a significant enough estate for the owner to adopt the place-name as the family name, despite having extensive holdings elsewhere, for example at Broxham, in the Weald. Apuldrefield manor was noted in AD1254 as gaining the right to hold a fair and market (Hasted, 1801:69), and further acquired the right to free-warren in AD1318. It had its own free chapel by AD1365, although this went out of use in the sixteenth century. The rights to certain lands, totalling 221 acres, 'lying dispersed within the bounds of this parish' (Hasted, 1801:76), but anciently belonging to the manor of 'Apulderfeld', were held in AD1371 by the prior and convent of Rochester. The estate was split up in the post-Medieval period and survives within the parish of Cudham as the place-name Aperfield. The manor house, comprising at least two chambers, a parlour and kitchen, was leased to a local yeoman in AD1641.

The exact location of the third manor of Bertrede is a matter of conjecture, although it is assumed to relate to the modern settlement of Berry's Green. Although noted in the IPM of AD1272 as belonging to Cudham, by c. AD1322 Bertrede had been annexed to Apuldrefield. Nevertheless, Bertrede was the venue for an annual fair from AD1334, although Hasted notes (1801:72) that its name was extinct by AD1380. It is therefore tempting to suggest that this was a settlement that was no longer viable after localised de-population caused by the Black Death of the mid-fourteenth century. A fourth manor also occurs in the documentary sources, that of Northsted, which straddled the boundary of Cudham and the neighbouring parish of Chelsfield to the north (Steinman, 1851).

The later Medieval documentary sources suggest both expansion and contraction of settlement within the parish, allied to a vigorous economy. Land ownership at the manorial level appears to have been flexible, especially evidenced by the dismantling of the minor manor of Bertrede in the late fourteenth century. The status of the right to hunt was high, with parks were attached to each individual manor. Unfortunately, these documentary sources are unable to give any significant indication of the location and extent of woodland features and are more muted on the matter of the land holdings and commons of the free peasantry. A list of field names generated from documentary sources for all the manors of

Cudham is presented in Appendix 2 and is discussed under the section on place-name evidence.

The post-Medieval history of Cudham is likewise under-researched. The various tracts of land within the parish became part of the holdings of different large estates. Steinman notes (1851:3) the transfer in AD1707, by the Lennard family, of a 383 acre farm known as Cudham Court, and the conveyance of 'the demesne lands of the manor, with the manor house (?) called Cudham Lodge' in AD1717 to the Stanhopes of Chevening.

Hasted remarks on the amount of coppice wood evident in the late eighteenth century, a comment which is echoed by Thorne's assertion of Cudham Woods, 'with a wild and solitary aspect', stretching intact through the heart of the parish fifty years earlier (1876:138). These woods had been cleared by AD1876 for cornfields, hop gardens and market gardens supplying soft fruit to London.

The documentary evidence illustrates the changing economic strengths of Cudham. In the eleventh century it might be characterised as a remote wooded place dependent economically in the main on arable agriculture and little affected by ongoing political changes. This might be contrasted with the vigour of the fourteenth century, with new settlements and wealth perhaps founded on woodland resources and land rents. In the post-Medieval period, in further contrast, it appears to be subsumed within a wider spectrum of land ownership, but itself remained marginalised and unchanging until the upheavals of the twentieth century. The extent to which Cudham is identifiable as a unique palimpsest of the processes dictated by the emergence of London at the centre, with the North Downs, amongst other places, on its periphery, is conjectural. This issue is addressed further below through the medium of the place-name evidence and through an analysis of the archaeological remains of the woodlands.

THE ARCHAEOLOGICAL EVIDENCE FOR SETTLEMENT AND LAND USE IN CUDHAM AND ENVIRONS

The lack of archaeological research within the parish of Cudham is reflected in the paucity of entries for it in the Sites and Monuments Record (SMR) for Greater London and in the National Sites and Monuments Record (NMR). What remains to record Cudham's development are its present topography and the ranges of earthworks, generally described as woodbanks, with their associated pollards and coppices. Indeed, woodbanks as a class of monument are poorly represented in the archaeological records of Greater London and their potential significance has not therefore been generally recognised. Nevertheless, archaeological investigations of the surrounding area of the North Downs and its dip-slope, taken together with artefact finds within the parish, provide a context within which a discussion of Cudham's woodlands can be set.

Little evidence has been found of Palaeolithic and Mesolithic period activity in this part of the North Downs, apart from a small number of flint implements found near Biggin Hill (Cotton, 1995). Neolithic early farmers occupied lowland sites on the north edge of the Downs, for example at Baston Manor, Hayes, (Philp, 1973) and in the Upper Cray Valley (ODAS, 1993a). Clarke (1982:25) indicates that clearance on the Downs may have occurred by the middle of third millennium BC, but also notes evidence of Neolithic activity within woodland environments. Axes made from local flint have occasionally been found, including a small number made from rocks quarried in Cornwall and Cumbria (Orpington and District Archaeological Society, 1993a:5).

Bronze Age settlements have also been found along the northern spring line of the Downs, extending westwards into modern day Surrey, for example at Carshalton, Beddington and Wallington (Needham, 1987:129). Small scale systems of square or rectangular fields have been noted in association with these, for example at Farthing Down, 10km to the west of Cudham (Needham, 1987:129). There are, however, no recorded finds or sites in the Cudham area for the period c3200BC to 700BC (Orpington and District Archaeological Society, 1993a). Needham concludes (1987:128) that there is little indication of intensive occupation of the North Downs, in contrast to the archaeological evidence for occupation of the chalklands of Wessex and Sussex.

Iron Age settlements have been found away from the high chalk zone, for example at Pilgrim's Way, Westerham (Philp, 1973), at the foot of the Downs to the south of Cudham, and the *oppidum* of Oldbury, 14km to the south east. The most significant Iron Age site in this area of the Downs is the enclosure at Caesar's Camp, Keston, to the north of Cudham. Situated on the slopes to the east of the Biggin Hill Valley, on a general north-south orientation and at a height of approximately 130m to 150m above OD, it commanded a low level route through the Downs and the other, east-west routeways. Barry Cunliffe indicates (1982:48) that it lay on the eastern limit of the hillfort zone of lowland Britain, and dominated a regional socio-economic territory that extended from Holmesdale in the south to the Thames in the north. Dated to c.200BC, Caesar's Camp comprises a triple earthen bank with a fighting platform within, and covers 1.2ha (Orpington and District Archaeological Society, 1993b). It is comparable in size to, for example, the hillforts of Gussage All Saints, Dorset and Little Woodbury in Wiltshire.

Fortunately for this study, the archaeological excavations on this site carried out in the late 1950s included pollen analyses. These indicated the range of vegetation that was present at the time of the enclosure's construction. Dimbleby states (1970:197)

... up to the time when the first stage of the inner rampart was constructed, the site had been covered with dense oak forest. Hazel, birch and holly were associated with oak, and there was some bracken there, but the light demanding grasses and heather were absent...this condition of high forest had existed for a long time - probably centuries. The rampart material overlying the buried soil... showed the heterogeneousness typical of made-up or disturbed soil. The woody species were still dominant, but the layers differed in the proportions of heather, grass, oak and birch pollen: in fact, the relatively high amount of heather and grass pollen...suggests that this material was brought to the site from some place where the forest was more open.

Whatever other contemporary sites that may have been in the vicinity have probably been ploughed out during the twentieth century, although an unenclosed settlement site was excavated at nearby Warbank and was found to include pits and four post structures (Crozier and Philp, 1985). Flinders-Petrie proposed to inspect places with the element *bury*, meaning camp or fort, in their place-names, seeking evidence of Iron Age earthworks and had proposed to examine, amongst others, Bury's Farm in Cudham (1880:11). The single recorded find from the Late Pre-Roman Iron Age in Cudham is a gold coin found in the vicinity of Berry's Green (Roach Smith, 1863). It bears an inscription of Cunobelinus, the tribal leader of the Catuvellauni, with, as the place of origin, the *oppidum* of Camulodunum (near modern day Colchester).

There is archaeological evidence to suggest that the North Downs were encroached upon during the Romano-British period (AD43 to AD410). A series of sites in the Hayes, West Wickham and Keston areas were excavated in the1960s (discussed by Philp, 1973). These are concentrated along the spring line of the Downs and on river gravels, for example, at Lower Warbank, Keston. Settlement evidence has also been found higher up on the Downs. The sites at Layhams Road and Highams Hill are on the clay with flint soil on the hilltop overlooking the Biggin Hill valley, at an elevation over 150m and near the arterial Roman road between London and Lewes. Of short duration in the second half of the first or early second century AD, the slight remains of these settlements indicate wood, wattle and daub structures of small farmsteads that might have made little impact on the subsequent pattern of the landscape (Philp, 1973:78-9).

The role of villa estates in opening up new lands for agriculture is commented on by Bird (1987:178). Substantial villa complexes are known to have existed in the lower lying areas, such as that at Lullingstone in the Darenth valley. These often stood in an, as yet undefined, relationship to earlier Pre-Roman settlements, for example the hill fort at Hulberry, 1km north-west of Lullingstone villa. It is suggested that villas do not occur much above the 50m contour in Kent, Surrey and Sussex (Sheldon et al, 1993). However, this assertion may be refuted by the discovery of an early Romano-British villa site situated above the 140m contour in the parish of Downe, adjacent to Cudham (MOLAS, work in progress). Studies of the landscape around the Barton Court Farm Roman villa site near Abingdon, Oxfordshire suggest the existence of a mixed oak-hazel coppice within 3km of that settlement (Miles and Branigan, 1986:72). If this small scale core/periphery model is correct, that places woodlands on the edge of a settlement's resource base in the Roman period, it is feasible that the woodlands extant in Downe and Cudham may have had their origins as the directly managed resources of Romano-British settlements situated on the

Downs, or indeed of earlier settlements, if continuity of land-use from the Pre-Roman Iron Age is demonstrable.

As yet, there are no direct indications of early Anglo-Saxon settlement in Cudham. However, the excavation of a sunken-featured building at Lower Warbank, Keston (Philp,1973:156-63), tentatively dated to AD450-550, suggests re-occupation of the Roman villa site at the northern approach to the Biggin Hill valley. Analyses of the bones on the site indicate 'a pastoral form of farming ... with sheep providing both meat for eating and wool for weaving' (Philp, 1973:159). This archaeological evidence may well indicate that the Cudham area of the Downs formed part of the 'complex transhumance grazing systems of the earlier Middle Ages' (Blair,1991:6) that particularly emphasised the north-south linearities noted in early Medieval Surrey. Alan Everitt (1986:171) notes the incidence of *stede* place-name elements in and around Cudham, which may also indicate their origins as sheep pastures.

The pottery on the Lower Warbank site was noted as 'resembling material from Saxon sites along the Thames estuary' (Philp, 1973:159). The inference of colonisation by Anglo-Saxon migrants from the Thames Valley, rather from Jutish Kent to the east (Evison, 1965), is further supported by cemetery evidence locally. The assemblages from Orpington Anglo-Saxon cemetery (8km north from Cudham church), dated to the period AD450-550, closely resemble those from cemetery sites much farther to the west (Tester, 1969:149). The grave goods from Polhill cemetery, 6km to the east on the edge of the Downs above the Darenth valley, dated by Brian Philp (1973:164) to AD650-750, reflect an undistinguished community, with few outstanding artifacts when compared to contemporary east Kentish seventh century graves at Dover Buckland (Evison, 1987). Analysis of the Polhill grave goods does indicate, however, a diverse range of artefacts, with parallels to goods found in East Kent, the Thames Valley and Hampshire (see Hawkes, 1973:187-191 for discussion on spears, seaxes and brooches from this site). The cemetery evidence might be taken to indicate that the Downlands were permanently settled by the seventh to eighth centuries, with links to a wider world. By extension of this argument, the pattern of land use, and in particular the formation of the managed woodscape as it is now evidenced, might date from such a period of permanent occupation. This evidence appears to corroborate Hewlett's assertion, based on analysis of hedgerow species, that the neighbouring parish of Chelsham was settled in the Saxon period in woodland clearings around its church (1980:95).

Before summation of this discussion of the early Medieval archaeology in this area of the North Downs, it is necessary to consider the routeways that intercut and define the parish of Cudham. The current parish boundary along its southernmost edge is partly coincident with the North Downs Way long distance footpath, following the scarp of the Downs to the English Channel at Dover. It's provenance as an ancient trackway is contested, however. Taylor (1979:7) suggests that 'the (North Downs) ridgeway ... was a possible line taken by Neolithic chert traders from the Isle of Portland'. In contrast, Turner (1980:1-12) comprehensively refutes the idea of an east-west routeway along the Downs in any period. He suggests that low level routes were more likely during the Pre-Roman Iron Age (600BC-AD50), along the dip-slope edge to the north of the Downs and the valley of Holmesdale to the south. The Roman road from London to Lewes across the Weald has already been noted, running on high ground, but is intercut by a perhaps earlier east-west trackway, which joins onto the north-south route through the Biggin Hill Valley. Poulton (1987:215) suggests that the boundary between Surrey and Kent was established to coincide with the line of the Roman road by AD700, although it also forms the western boundary of the diocese of Rochester, founded earlier in AD604.

The main lines of travel were on a north-south axis, which in the pre-Conquest period were probably the droveways of swineherds, migrating with their herds from the settlements north of the Downs to their detached pasture lands in the Weald (Everitt, 1986:36). These are identifiable in the landscape as occurring approximately every kilometre along the escarpment and with steep gradients. A direct line on a map is discernible from Cudham to the outlier manor at Marsh Green, which may also have been used for summer grazing. Interleaved with these cross-country routes are lanes and hollow ways that Everitt (1986:268) suggests 'must often have arisen as local forest footpaths trodden out between one pasture or farmstead and another during the Old English period or after the Conquest'.

This discussion of the archaeological evidence has attempted to provide a context for analysis of the settlement and land use of Cudham in the pre-Conquest period. In terms of archaeological research, the North Downs might be characterised as the dull sister of the more glamorous South Downs and have been neglected accordingly. Current archaeological evidence suggests that the North Downs were passed through and intermittently used until more permanent occupation occurred, from perhaps the 8th century onwards. It was this phase of settlement that may have prompted the clearance of the woodlands. Earlier systems of land use may have been subsumed within the more intensive structuring of the landscape practised by early Medieval settlers. Forms of woodland management incorporating substantial bankings are perhaps unlikely to pre-date the Anglo-Saxon settlement of the North Downs.

Sites and finds for the later Medieval period are similarly scarce. The church of St Peter and St Paul is the main representative for this period. Everitt (1986:195) suggests that it may have originated as a daughter church of Orpington, in a phase of early Anglo-Saxon expansion along and up the Downs, with churches established on the private 'booklands' of the local thegn. Situated near to the parish boundary, the church is centrally placed on the north-south axis of the Downs, at the conjunction of the main routes through the eastern part of the parish. The spire is clearly visible from both the northern and southern ends of the parish, but is scarcely in evidence from any other perspective. According to the church guide of 1955, the earliest part of the structure is thought to be the South or Warrior chapel, together with a portion of the tower. The nave is possibly Saxo-Norman, with a semi-circular apse at the eastern end that was replaced by a chancel c.AD1250. An additional chapel to St. Katherine was built on the north side of the nave in AD1350, that is, contemporary with the Black Death (1348-51), although a linking of these two events must remain speculative. The Norman tower contains a peal of bells, the oldest of which is dated to AD1490. The church fabric was much refurbished in the nineteenth and twentieth centuries (Gander, unpub.). A single sixteenth century memorial brass to Alys Waleys records her as the wife of a resident of the village. The church does not appear to have been richly furnished in any period or to have been extensively rebuilt, apart from occasional endowments.

The churchyard is approximately 105m by 60m, and is roughly oval in shape. The church is sited adjacent to two yew trees, which stand 30m apart on an east-west axis. The westerly, male tree has been estimated as being 1500 years old, with the easterly female estimated at 2000 years old (Meredith, 1984). Aston argues that many of the small churches of the late Saxon period 'were no doubt replacements for periodic meetings at pagan sites' (1985:49). The conjunction of the major trackways, the church, the yews and the hall, with the latter on the south side of the church, suggests a symbolic appropriation of an important place by the Anglo-Saxon, Christian owners of the Downland settlements.

The current fabric of Cudham Court is of post-Medieval origin, as indeed are most of the buildings within the parish. The exceptions are isolated farmhouses, such as Bombers Farm and Hostye Farm, which include some timber framing within later structures that might be dated to the fifteenth century. A moated site was discovered and then destroyed during the construction of Aperfield Court, in the early nineteenth century (Nelson, 1982:15). Turner (1987:230), discussing moated sites in Medieval Surrey, notes that most date to the period AD1200-1350, but that their existence declined sharply after the Black Death. Although generally small and square in shape, moats are posited as indicating fashionable and social status, rather than having a purely practical application. There are ribbons of flint-faced, post-Medieval buildings along the main routes through the parish, principally around Cudham, Horns Green and Leaves Green. There is, however, no evidence of settlement nucleation anywhere in the parish before the early modern period.

AERIAL PHOTOGRAPHS

Three sets of vertical aerial photographs of the parish, taken June 1971, October 1986 and August 1991, are available for consultation in Bromley local Studies library. Grubbed out woodlands were visible in outline on all of these photos, but they did not extend the range noted from the 1871 OS map. No other archaeological features are determinable from them, although the fields around Hostye Farm (TQ446606) do have anomalous marks running across them that could not be linked to known earlier field boundaries.

THE WOODLANDS OF CUDHAM

PLACE-NAMES IN CUDHAM PARISH

The place-name Cudham suggests an Anglo-Saxon origin. It has been variously interpreted as meaning the homestead or village of a man named Cuda (Mills, 1991:99); a combination of the Celtic word *coed* for woodland and *hām* for enclosure (Kinnibrugh,1976:8), although this particular interpretation is vigorously disputed by Paul Cullen (pers. comm.); or a topographical term, from an OE cognate of the Old Frisian *kuda* (and of German dialect **käutel** 'swelling), also evidenced in OE **codd** 'bag', denoting the rounded shape of the down (Wallenberg, 1931:361). OE *hām* 'homestead, village' is an important term in Kentish place-names.

Post-Medieval settlements in the parish also have names that reflect on the woodlands and Medieval land use. Biggin Hill has been interpreted as meaning 'the hill near the dwelling' (Wallenberg, 1934:23), derived from ME **bigging** 'building', although the root of this word is Scandinavian and may not have relevance here. If the Biggin Hill valley was a place of early settlement, then the hill above it might conceivably be so named. Wallenberg also provides an alternative meaning (1934:23), suggesting a connection to Robert *Bygge* de Codeham, named in a document of AD1292. When standing in the valley on the north-south trackway and looking up, a translation as 'a hill that bends' derived perhaps from **bygan** appears equally apt. Paul Cullen comments (Pers. Comm.) that an earlier form of the name, given as *Byggynheld* in a document of AD1440, demonstrates that the second element is the OE **helde** 'slope' rather than **hyll** 'hill'. He suggests that the first element is actually derived from an OE term for 'beacon'. Given the siting of this place on a high point on the North Downs, with clear sight lines to the north northwest and the Thames valley west of the urban centre of London, this explanation is perhaps the most plausible. In this context it is important to refer again to the Saxon cultural material in the nearby seventh century inhumation cemetery at Polhill, suggesting that the Biggin Hill valley may have provided an access route for that material. Supporting evidence for the 'beacon' explanation also includes a field-name 'Beacon Shaw' at the south west of the parish further up the Biggin Hill valley route through the Downs. It is also noted that there is a Biggin Wood in modern Upper Norwood (North Wood) on the next highest range of hills to the north and that it is possibly visible from Biggin Hill itself. A brief consideration of the distribution of *Biggin* place-names in the Greater London area locates them only in the southwest sector, with additional examples at Mitcham and Kingston upon Thames, suggesting a putative network of beacons linking visibly the communities on the North Downs to those in the Thames Valley, possibly in the period before the Norman Conquest.

The settlements with the place-names of Berry's Green, Leaves Green and Horns Green are all situated around the perimeter of the parish. Berry's Green has an unclear locational relationship with the Medieval manor of Bertrede. The place-name Bertrede might be interpreted as a combination of *bury* (following Flinders-Petrie's suggestion), meaning defended enclosure, and *rede*, meaning clearing or ridden through a wood. A document of AD1360 gives *Northberden* and *Southberden*, but it is the combined meaning of the elements **ber-** and **denn** together that remain obscure. The second element could be either OE **denu** 'long two-sided valley' or **denn** 'woodland pasture'. Possible meanings of the first element are OE **bere** 'barley', **b□r** '(woodland) pasture, **bær** 'bare, without vegetation' and, indeed, **by:re** 'byre, cowshed' as well as indicating a number of personal names (Paul

Cullen, pers. comm.). Nevertheless, the woodlands associations of this place-name are clear.

Leaves Green straddles the parish boundary with Keston to the north, with a name possibly derived from **leays**, meaning glade or pasture. Horn's Green is located near to Cudham Frith, on the eastern boundary of the parish, its name meaning corner. Roden has commented with reference to the Chilterns (1968:68) that '...small patches of common wood ... were being reduced to 'greens' in the later Middle Ages, by felling and grazing'. These predominantly post-Medieval settlements might therefore represent the location of the common woods of the parish, rather than the location of the earlier settlements.

MAPS OF CUDHAM PARISH

Unfortunately, there is no Anglo-Saxon charter for the parish nor any further, unpublished, Medieval documents, leaving only post-Medieval maps as a major source of evidence about changes to the woodlands of Cudham. These maps are available at Bromley Local History Library and the Kent County Records Office in Maidstone and include:

- The 1838 Tithe map of Cudham and its complete list of apportionments
- A map of the parish of Cudham, dating to 1788
- An estate map of Hostye Farm (Area 4), dated to 1714 (U908 P77/1)
- An estate map of the manor of Cudham Court Lodge (Area 4), dated to 1686 (U908 P76).

The last three maps varied considerably in style, despite overlapping both temporally and spatially. When compared with the very detailed estate map of 1714, the whole parish map exhibited a neatened version of the woodlands, with extant shaws erased. This comparative exercise emphasised the value of considering a range of map sources together, whilst bearing in mind the various purposes behind the original drawing of the maps. These might have included the provision of an accurate representation of land use or to produce a map that glorified the landscape in line with prevailing attitudes. In this sense, the Tithe map, by virtue of the intensity of detailing that it encompasses, is a more consistent source, albeit of a later date. By tacking between maps, particular anomalies noted in the fieldwork phase of the research could be clarified.

An example of one such anomaly is a small flint-banked area at the northern edge of Shieling Field (see analysis of Area 3). This appears to be relatively recent as it is not shown on the tithe map and consists of a modern coppice plantation. However, it is clearly shown on the 1788 map, and indicates post-Medieval banking which might then be compared to others of a similar form in the parish. The notable feature of this comparative mapping exercise was the strong degree of continuity between the maps regarding field boundaries.

The value of the tithe apportionment document to any detailed landscape study is that it lists the name and acreage of each land parcel, the ownership and occupation, the land value and the current usage. For Cudham, the Tithe map details field edges with a taxable value, these occurring as wooded shaws or areas of rough. When the Tithe map was compared with the 6" to the mile 1871 Ordnance survey map, it was evident that, in the period between their production, a significant part of Cudham Lodge Wood (Area 2) had been converted to fields, but that otherwise there was continuity between the wooded areas shown. As a resource for the project methodology, the 1400 tithe apportionments were annotated onto the 1871 OS map, drawing in those boundaries that had been lost as fields were amalgamated for arable agriculture. This exercise produced a map that identified by name every part of the landscape, to which the woodbanks could then be related.

In practice, it would have been a labour-intensive and unwieldy exercise to search the field name evidence for the whole parish without the benefit of computer software. (The entry of tithe map information into readily available computer manipulated databases is, of course, now underway nationally, with many available via the Public Records Office). The problem was resolved by searching the tithe apportionments for specific terms, based on the glossary of terms presented as Appendix 3. The assumption was made that there might be a perpetuation of Medieval land plot names into the modern period. The field names were searched for the following sets and then related back to the composite 1871 Ordnance Survey and Tithe map.

1) All woodland names, such as 'coppice', 'grove', 'wood' and 'shaw' and those indicating past uses, for example 'wood field', that is, a field cut from a wood.

2) All enclosure names, particularly 'crofts', 'tyes', 'hursts', 'leys' and 'haughs'.

3) Any names indicating specific activities relating to woodland products

4) Open field names that might relate to the extensive ploughlands noted in the Domesday Book reference

From this evidence, used in conjunction with the fieldwork results, phased maps of land use in Cudham were produced. These were then interpreted to discuss the dominance throughout the historic period of the production of marketable surpluses from woodlands, As part of this exercise, the list of field names generated from the documentary sources (Appendix 2) was compared with the tithe names. There was indeed a continuity of names, with, for example, Hazel Wood being a rare intact survivor into the twentieth century.

The findings from this research exercise are presented below and are ordered by area. The numbers in brackets denote the tithe apportionment number for that piece of land.

Area 1
Based on the assumption that shaws are remnants of areas of woodland, it appears, from connecting up shaws on the 1871/tithe map, that this area had been extensively wooded in the past. The wooded areas are generally high on the valley sides and on the clay with flint plateau. More recent fields, with regular shapes and names relating to their size, for example Eight Acre field, have been cut out of them.

The occurrence of croft names in area 1 is exclusively on the clay with flint, with the single exception of the Lord's Croft. This land parcel lies on the chalk area that abuts the alluvial deposit at the bottom of the Biggin Hill valley. The problematic nature of the soil type here is attested by the adjacent field name of 'Good for nothing'. Hewlett (1980:96) asserts that the chalk valleys in neighbouring Chelsham were first enclosed in the fourteenth century.

There is a cluster of three crofts around Skid Hill Farm (these are discussed further below). Wallenberg (1934:23) gives a place-name meaning for Skid that is derived from *scid*, or a thin slip of wood, shingle or billet. The name 'Schidden' given in a document of AD1371 incorporates either **denu** or **denn** (see above) as a second element. A second tranche of 'skid' names occurs further to the south, to the northwest of the extant Long Coppice, but on the clay with flint soil. Field names containing the *scid* element only occur in this sector of the parish. Paul Cullen remarks that the element may also survive in 'sheeting' field names in the parish (pers. comm.)

Between Skid Hill and Jewels Wood (1) are field names associated with leather tanning, for example Great Tanning Bottom. These named fields occur on both the chalk and the clay with flint. Oak bark is used in tanning processes and oak is an easily cleavable material, from which *scids* could have been produced (Hodges,1989:121) therefore suggesting the presence of extensive oak woodlands in this area that were managed as a resource. Their period of use and the timing of their subsequent clearance are unknown. The association remains, however, in the name of the trackway running along the valley floor, now known as Oaklands Lane, but previously called Colliers Lane, relating to the production of charcoal.

At the southern, higher end of area 1, Shepherds Haw is noted abutting the Roman road and is discussed later with other 'haw' named fields. All field boundaries along the Roman road abut it and are not cut by it, therefore confirming a post-Roman date of field patterning. Amongst the fields adjacent to Shepherds Haw, the element 'ground' is dominant. John Field (1993:19) considers this term to denote large pastures that were enclosed in the fifteenth or sixteenth centuries.

On the east side of the Biggin Hill valley, on the opposite side to Jewels Wood but adjacent to the Keston-Tatsfield road, are two 'leys'. Further examples are to be found adjacent to the Roman road where it is intersected by the east-west trackway.

The complex of tithe names around Mollards Wood (wood number 2 on the Woodlands of Cudham map) is presented here as a case study (see fig.5). A croft, or small enclosure often associated with a dwelling (Field, 1993), of irregular shape (Tithe map number 95), abuts the Roman road and appears to have been cut from the woodland, evidenced by a sinuous boundary line. As no other tracks lead to it, it is suggested that this particular croft was a place of Anglo-Saxon settlement, contemporaneous with continued usage of the road in the post Roman period. The outline of an estate is perhaps discernible, bounded by the Roman road to the west, the meandering trackway, to the south east, that encloses Horn Hair (Tithe map number 73) (horn meaning corner, Field, 1993:142), the northern edge of Great Mallwood (Tithe map number 97) and the north-eastern edge of Jerry Ridden (Tithe map number 160). Fields Tithe map numbers 84 and 90 have been cut from the woods, perhaps for cattle pasturage, with the term 'land' indicating a late Medieval provenance. Cleared woodland, termed a ridden (Tithe map number 160), has been brought back into woodland use in a later phase (Tithe map number 163). The fields (Tithe map numbers 76 and 83) on the eastern side of the trackway may have been used for the production of billets. The field name Pedley Hazel (Tithe map number 105) indicates an area of coppice abutting the Roman road, perhaps in the ownership of Petley manor in Downe parish. The name Petley is evidenced there by documents from the fourteenth century onwards. A complex of fields around Kid Croft (Tithe map number 141), including further 'horn' names, suggests another discrete land holding.

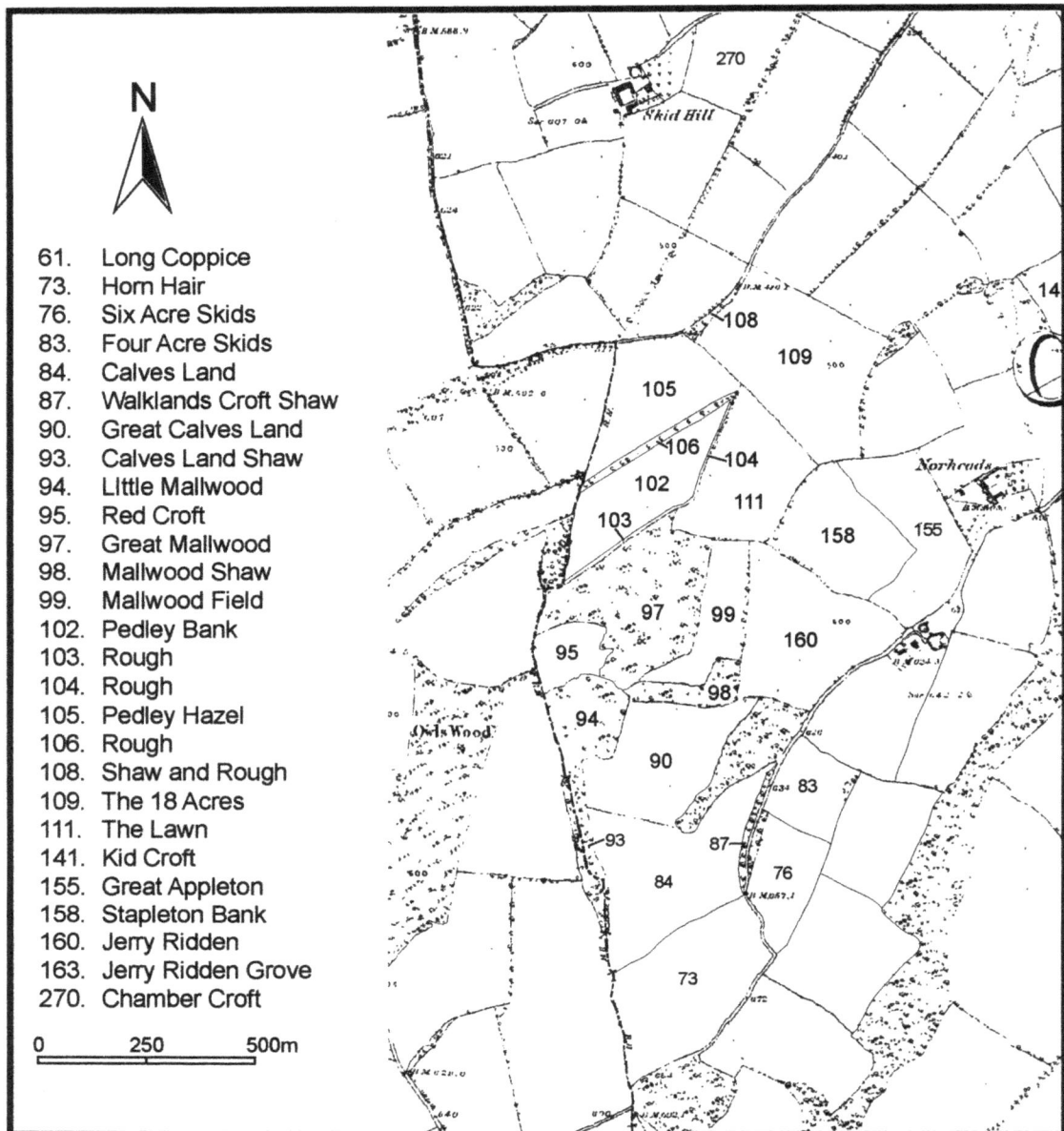

N

61. Long Coppice
73. Horn Hair
76. Six Acre Skids
83. Four Acre Skids
84. Calves Land
87. Walklands Croft Shaw
90. Great Calves Land
93. Calves Land Shaw
94. Little Mallwood
95. Red Croft
97. Great Mallwood
98. Mallwood Shaw
99. Mallwood Field
102. Pedley Bank
103. Rough
104. Rough
105. Pedley Hazel
106. Rough
108. Shaw and Rough
109. The 18 Acres
111. The Lawn
141. Kid Croft
155. Great Appleton
158. Stapleton Bank
160. Jerry Ridden
163. Jerry Ridden Grove
270. Chamber Croft

0   250   500m

FIGURE 5. CASE STUDY: MOLLARDS WOOD

Wallenberg (1934:530) suggests that place-names with the prefix 'moll' are derived from the Old English *mal* meaning action at law, bargaining, agreement or pay. He therefore interprets Mallwood as indicating woods for which rent was paid in commutation of labour dues. This suggests that the naming of this wood originates in the later Medieval period, unless the commutation of labour dues for rent was already in place locally before the Norman Conquest.

Area 2

The earlier extent of Cudham Lodge Wood is indicated by the tranche of post-Medieval straight edged fields with names indicating their acreage, which were probably cut from it and located to the south of Leaves Green in the area now covered by the Biggin Hill airfield. This wood appears to have extended over the whole of area 2, to the east of the present A233, in the later Medieval period. In the north-east corner of this section, and adjacent to a trackway running along the Downe side of the parish boundary, are four 'leys'. Their presence adds weight to Everitt's assertion (1986:148) that the place-name Leaves Green denotes an area of upland pasture.

The domination of Cudham Lodge Wood over this area of the parish may have dictated the distribution of other types of land use in the vicinity. The remnants of an open-field system are evident between the south west parish boundary, above Tatsfield, and the Keston-Westerham road (A233). The fields here have names with West, South, Priest and Lady as prefixes, further subdivided into Great and Little variants. Associated with this complex of fields are 'lands', perhaps cut from the wood adjacent to the north eastern side of this road, indicating an extension of arable farming in the later Medieval period. A windmill was sited between the open fields and the trackway to Aperfield manor. In directly geographical association with the manor house at Aperfield was the enclosure called Great Tye, one of only two instances of this name element in the entire parish. The element 'tye' in field names is limited to the south eastern counties of England and is confined locally to east Surrey (Field, 1993:24).

Seven crofts names are present in area 2, all of them dispersed along the main route ways on clay with flint soils. Post-Medieval coppice and woodland plantations are noted in the southernmost, and highest, part of this area. The steeply sloping area of woodland named Deadman's Bank may conceivably be the site of a later Anglo-Saxon burial ground for executed criminals. Its location fits with that described by Andrew Reynolds (1998) for these sites, that is within sight of important communication routes and lying on a boundary, in this case, that of the parish, the county and the hundred. Local folklore suggests alternatively that the name is derived from the adjacent field of Denman's Bottom and apocryphal stories of murder and tragic death (Nelson, 1982:124).

Area 3

The largest coherent piece of woodland here is Cudham Frith. The term 'frith' is common on the Downs and denotes a pre - Conquest wood. This section of the parish is characterised in the main by significantly smaller land plots. Many lack specific names and are surrounded by woodland and shaws. The sinuous outline of Buckhurst, meaning 'beech tree wood' (Wallenberg, 1934:23), and containing an unnamed enclosure, suggests a pre - Conquest area of woodland.

Other field names may have particular importance for the mapping of the earliest pre – Conquest use and settlement of this area of the Downs. A document of AD1247 names *Werland*, then a field of ten acres. The first element **wer** is ambiguous and offers insufficient evidence for a clear explanation, comments Paul Cullen (pers. comm.). Formal possibilities include a meaning of 'weir, river-dam', which is perhaps unlikely due to the absence of surface streams on the Downs. An alternative interpretation is as a derivation from OE **wer(e)** '?guard, ?lookout'. The closest extant field name to which this might relate is Woollards Hill, which is situated directly opposite to the church and at the intersection of the major north-south and east-west trackways. This field is on a steep slope on the eastern side of a deep north-south orientated dry valley, with good visual aspect and mirrors in this respect *Byggynheld* discussed earlier. Fields adjacent to Woollards Hill have been renamed, in the post-Medieval period, in the ownership of the Hicks family of New Barn Farm. The name New Barn may itself be a corruption of New Bourne, as indicated on an earlier map, perhaps hinting that flowing water was extant here in earlier periods. Adjacent to New Barn Farm further up this same valley and on a slope is the small field currently known as Kemp Hill, probably the one named *Kempeheld* in a document of AD1440. The first element is probably the surname *Kemp(e)*, itself derived from the OE *cempa* 'warrior' and ME *kempe* 'warrior, athlete, wrestler' (Paul Cullen, pers. comm.).

Horns Croft, in the south-western corner of this section, appears to be a small farmstead in origin, associated with Broomcocks Wood. It is defined on two sides by the road and the parish boundary. Alder Haugh, between Grays Wood and Cudham Frith is situated on a clay with flint promontory between two chalk valleys (discussed further in the fieldwork report). Adjacent to it is a shieling, indicating its use as summer pasture. The proximity to Silversted farm and a pond is noted. Woodlands with personal names attached indicate probable post-Medieval plantations in this area.

At the northern edge of the area near to the parish boundary is a second block of open field names. These are associated with an enclosure named Old Haugh and abut a particularly meandering stretch of road that traverses a level area of terrain. Around Berrys Green there were no field names that could be related to the list of Bertrede manor tithe field names, taken from an earlier document but published in 1804 (Gomme, 1898), further suggesting that this was rather the site of communal woodlands (see above) and that the short-lived manor proper lay further to the north, perhaps nearer to the modern Single Street. Hemplands, a communal field for the growing of hemp for rope and commonly sited near to dwellings (Field,1993:99), is situated at the junction of three trackways across the parish.

Area 4
The tithe map shows many subdivisions within the woods here, for example within Great Molloms Wood (another incidence of *mal* land) and Homefield Spring. Dens and leys surrounded by shaws are again found in the northernmost, lower part of the parish. A total of nine crofts are distributed along the two main trackways that lead up to the church. Their distance from the church highlights the dispersed settlement pattern throughout the Medieval period. The fourth 'haugh' name field of the parish, Alder Haw, is located between the trackways, but appears to be associated with a cluster of leys, sinuous trackways and fields cut from tracts of woodland. A cluster of fields centred on Hostye Farm suggests elements of an open field system, these possibly being the demesne lands of Cudham manor. Two field names including warren as a component suggest that the Medieval hunting range lay in the area parallel to the north eastern boundary of the parish, on the western flank of the Norstead valley.

The incidence of personal names for woods and the very piecemeal nature of the woodscape perhaps indicate land changing usage over time, from wood to arable and back again. The field shapes appear to be consistent with assarting, but this is contradicted by the place name evidence. This suggests that the main elements of the extant woodland are late Medieval at the earliest.

The problem of over reliance on place name evidence is illustrated by the case study presented in fig. 6. This study is a comparison of a map of AD1714 and the composite 1838/1871 tithe/Ordnance Survey map for the same area to the north of Hostye farm. Places lose names as well as gain them. Earlier names are masked by later agricultural regimes, for example the earlier crofts hidden within the Fifteen Acre field. Changing ownership changes association of parts, for example the Southfield shaw became part of another landholding. Hazel Wood and the White croft are the only evidenced examples of cultivated groves in the parish, as identified by Roden (1968) in the Chilterns. On the original of the AD1714 map, the area O (paddock) indicated a cultivated grove within a wood pasture.

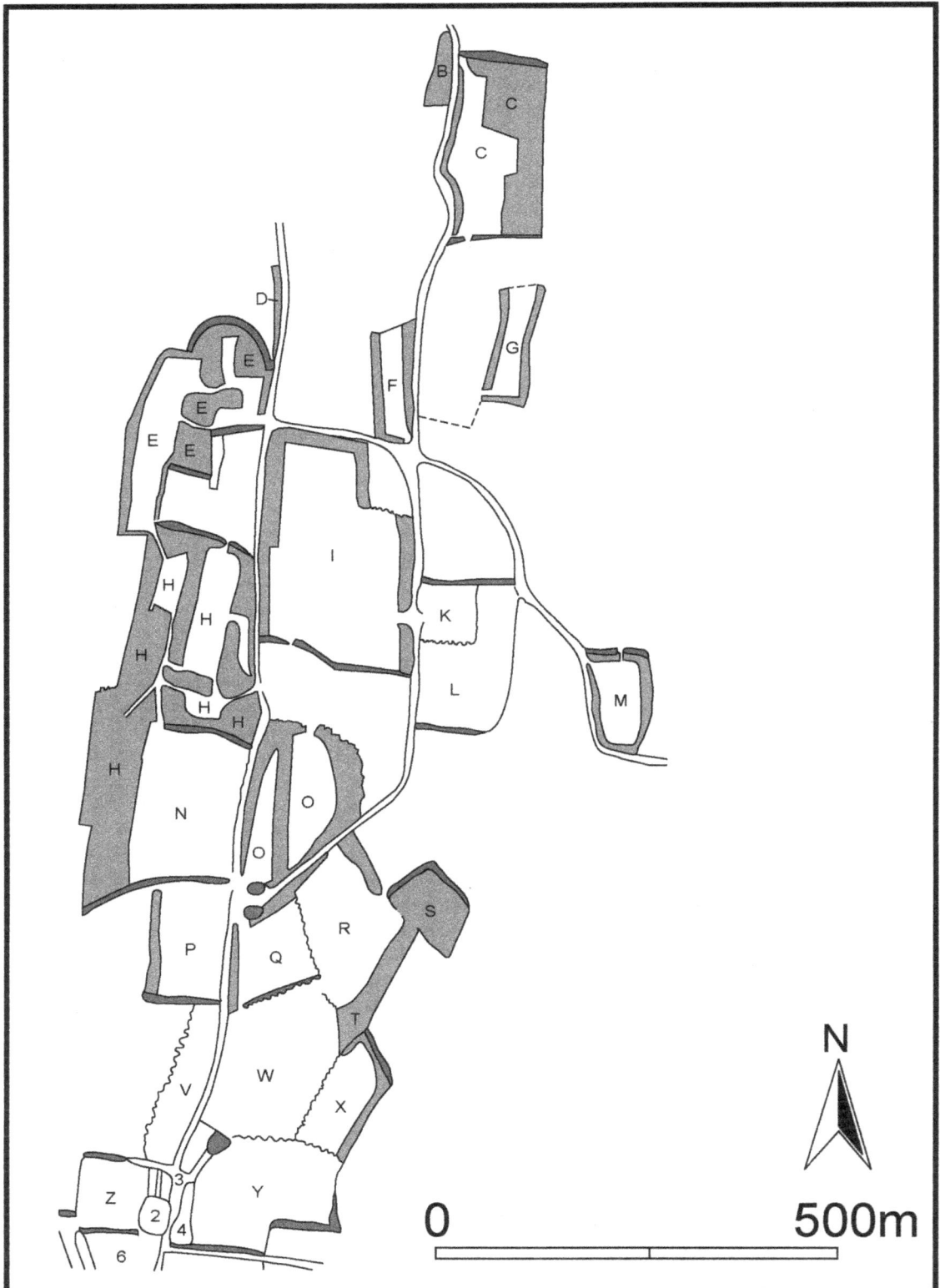

FIGURE 6. HOSTYE FARM: ESTATE MAP AND TITHE MAP COMPARISON

B.	Haukins West Shaw	Haukins Shaw West
C.	Great Haukings	Haukins Wood
D.	Cony Earth	Gypsies Walk
E.	White Croft	White Croft
F.	Part of the Streak	un-named
G.	White Earth	White Earth
H.	Hards Dale	Lower Hazel & Hazel Wood
I.	Perre Croft	Lower & Upper Perry's Croft
K.	Mobs Hole	un-named
L.	Hell Grove	Hill Grove
M.	Allder Haw	Alder Haw
N.	Lower Hardsdale	Middle Hazel
O.	Paddock	Paddock
P.	Upper Hardsdale	Upper Hazel
Q.	Little Southfield	Southfield
R.	Great Southfield	Little Mount Hill
S.	Southfield Grove	Southfield Shaw
T.	Southfield Shaw	Hubbards Hill Shaw
V.	Long Croft	Long Croft
W.	Home Croft	The 15 Acres
X.	Colls Croft	The 15 Acres
Y.	The Mead	The Mead
Z.	Little Pound Field	Little Lord's Field

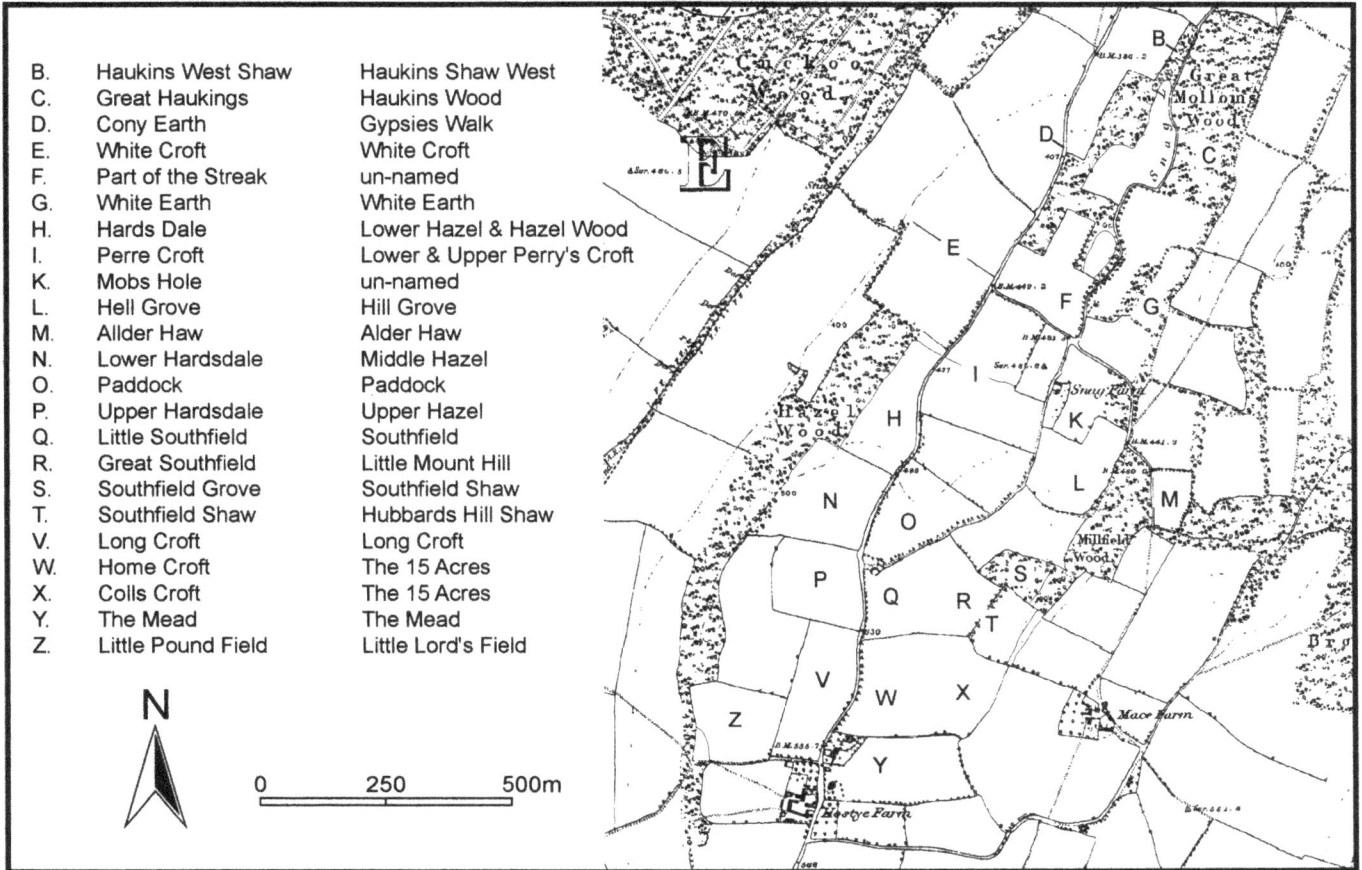

0   250   500m

TREE RECORDING STUDY

The aim of the tree recording exercise was to use the managed tree forms as potentially datable ecofacts, which could contribute to the overall analysis of phases of woodland use in Cudham. When noted in association with banks, the trees would indicate the latest date before which the banks were constructed. To this end, a total of 42 trees were noted on the Tree Recording Sheets, (the format of which is presented in Appendix 1). These trees were also annotated onto the field map, together with details of other recordable features, such as trees that had been laid into hedgerows and had subsequently grown out into misshapen standards. This latter group was predominantly in single species hedges of beech. Hewlett (1973:95) asserts that 'the heavy clay with flint areas on top of the hills support hedges which are mostly remnants of the original woodland cover and reflect the nature of this woodland closely'. It might be expected that ancient hedgerows would include a wider range of plant species, indicating that the beech hedgerows are more modern in origin.

The range of data recorded owes much to the work of Oliver Rackham and to the field guide *Woodland Archaeology in Surrey* (Bannister, 1996). These works have taken into account the particular environmental conditions that affected tree growth, for example, soil type and climate, and the visible results of human management, such as the crown growth of pollards occurring after their last cropping. The shape of the crown growth of a tree, if narrow and straight for example, might indicate that the tree had grown closely surrounded by others. If these trees are cleared away, then the crown of the tree left standing produces a diagnostic shape when it subsequently develops. The girth of standing trees was recorded where possible, usually at a height of 1.5m above the ground. The overall dimensions of selected coppice stools were also recorded.

Although a small number of trees from which to make assertions about the antiquity of the woodlands of Cudham, the distribution of the sample reflects the dispersed nature of the woodlands and the variety of forms throughout the parish. It was not possible to make a quantitative analysis of the density of woodlands from this sample, however. The trees recorded were located mainly on the surveyed banks and in hedgerows adjacent to footpaths. The fact of their recording was dictated by their relative accessibility. The results of this exercise are presented within the fieldwork reports for each area, subject to the following discussion of the methodological difficulties encountered in this phase of research.

The analysis of these ecofacts for age proved to be particularly problematic. Mitchell comments (1994:5) that Rackham's assertions of ages for trees are not supported by a means of calculating them. Patch (1994:5) highlights the difficulty of developing a reliable formula for dating humanly managed trees. The ages postulated below are therefore no more than a 'best guess' based on an interpretation of current knowledge. As this was a non-intrusive study, the determining evidence of counting annual growth rings was not available. Where possible the rings on the stumps of felled trees were counted, although this of course then gives little information as to the actual form of the tree under examination.

A sample of coppice stools, in Pimlico Wood and Cudham Frith, were recorded. No precise method of dating coppice stools could be ascertained from published work. Oliver Rackham suggests (1995a:15) that an ash stool on a good site might be 1.5m (5') across after 300 years. The poor soils and upland nature of Cudham's landscape perhaps preclude its definition as a good site, and in any case the main coppiced species still in evidence were beech and sweet chestnut. As a guideline, an estimate of 350 years of age for 1.5m of coppice stool length, regardless of species, was adopted.

A more accurate assessment might be achievable, however, through a synthesis of a wide range of evidence. Given the fact of coppice plantation in the eighteenth and nineteenth centuries, precise dates of planting for extant coppices might be established from map sources. There are certainly areas of relatively modern sweet chestnut coppice at Mace Farm, Cudham. Individual stools might be measured on plan for overall length and width. From a quantifiable sample, for example ten per cent of those present, taken from both within and on the edge of the wood, an average area of stool might be established. This could then be set against the known period of growth to establish a consistent ratio of size to age. This ratio could then be applied to areas of coppice of unknown date of origin. This method would have the advantage of comparing stools of the same species growing in the same environmental conditions. On the debit side, it does not take into account the changing lengths of the coppicing cycles and periods of dormancy that might have affected the overall size of the stool in different eras. Further work is required in this particular area before reliable estimates of age might be accepted.

The assessment of age for standards is based on an estimate of 1" of girth per year of growth (Mitchell, 1978:25). This estimate takes into account the differential growth rates throughout the life of a tree, but as a rule of thumb relates best to species of trees, such as oak, ash and beech, grown on optimum sites and achieving a full crown. Trees existing within restricted circumstances, such as within a wood or in an avenue, might be expected to grow at a slower rate. Yew trees are exceptional in the slowness of their girth expansion, with an estimate of 480 cm (16') representing 600-800 years (Mitchell, 1978:25).

Individual beech standards were recorded in significant positions, for example on the corner of a wood bank. Judging by the large rotten stumps found in such positions, many of the biggest trees in the parish were lost in the 1987 storm. The largest example, on the parish boundary adjacent to Dennley Bottom, (TQ424623) had a girth of 206", suggesting a date of planting in the late eighteenth century. This individual may well have been a pollard and therefore possibly significantly older. The general absence of large standards in locations other than in avenues and shaws reflects the clearance of the woodlands in Cudham in the past two hundred years. The largest individuals noted were probably the result of replanting in the early nineteenth century.

Pollards proved to be particularly problematic for assessing age. Comparable securely dated assemblages were sought by contacting the wardens of Epping Forest, Essex and Burnham Beeches, in the Chilterns, but none could be ascertained. The Forestry Authority Research Information Note 250 *Estimating the age of large trees in Britain* (1994) gives a formulaic approach, which takes into account changing growth patterns throughout the life of a tree. This generally accords with the 1" (2.5cm) of girth per year approach for common species suggested by Mitchell (1978:25). Unfortunately there is no data specifically relating to beech pollards, which formed the majority of those encountered in Cudham. The worked example of an oak pollard (FARIN, 1994) estimates an age of 393 years, based on a girth of 555cm (222"). This gives a factor of 1.77 times an inch of girth to estimate age in years. Based on the comparative annual ring growth rates of oak (4mm) and beech (5mm), taken from Table 1 of the Research note (p4), indicating that beeches grow at a slightly faster rate, a factor of 1.4 is suggested for beeches when pollarded.

Whilst not claimed as an rigid mathematical formula, this calculation does offer a plausible minimum age for pollards in the absence of alternatives.

All of the 22 beech pollards recorded had substantial crown growth since their last cropping. Time elapsed since this event was difficult to gauge. Rackham (1995a, plate XIII) shows pollards from Felbrigg, Norfolk, which he suggests were already ancient when last cut in the eighteenth century. These exhibit similar crown growth and girth to the line of seven pollards on the north edge of Great Molloms Wood, shown in photos 1 and 2. The average girth of this latter assemblage was 165" (smallest 107" but much overhung by its neighbours, largest 209"). The age of this line, based on the calculation outlined above, is estimated at 231 years (in 1997), planted in the mid eighteenth century. There is an obvious mis-match between these two sets of assertions for age. Another beech pollard, from a set that possibly marked the extent of the post-Medieval Cudham Lodge estate, possesses a high crown, grows on a clay with flint bank, and has a girth at 1.5m of 410cm (164"). Its estimated age is 230 years, that is, also planted in the mid eighteenth century. The map of Cudham parish of AD1788 indicates the Leaves Green Beeches running along this boundary. This suggests that these were already a significant feature by that time, and that their date of origin may have been at least 80 years earlier, that is, the length of time taken for a beech tree to reach maturity. Therefore it is possible to suggest that a beech pollard of girth 410cm is approximately a minimum of 300 years old. This forces a revised factor of 1.8 into the age calculation determined by girth, and revises the average ages of the Great Molloms Wood pollards as also approximately 300 years. The variations within this particular assemblage, given that all, bar the smallest which was in an anomalous position, can be asserted as being planted at the same time, highlights the problems of this approach. A group of trees living under the same conditions exhibit different rates of growth that allow ages to be calculated that are between 284 and 376 years, giving a statistical deviation of 28%.

It must also be suggested that the use of girth dimensions in relation to pollards is itself a possibly misleading exercise. Whilst standard tree trunks are of a roughly uniform circular shape, those of pollards, on close inspection, are much more uneven. The strands of the trunks are much more clearly related to their point of origin within the root system and form a much less homogenous whole, making girth measurements inaccurate. In addition, the measurement of girth taken at 1.5m above ground level often coincides with a narrowing of the trunk before it flowers upwards into the cropping area. Perhaps an error arises in treating pollards as standards, indicating that they might be better served when treated as elongated coppice stools. Indeed, their significant features, of vigorous and extensive root systems and horizontally expanding regenerative area, mirror stools far more closely than standards, and suggest the trunks as being a conduit for resources rather than an area of essential growth. These queries do not, however, resolve the question of assessing pollards for age. At best, a combination of documentary evidence for specific assemblages, together with detailed measurement of the circumference of the base of the latest growing area of those pollards still extant, might eventually produce a more reliable assessment.

The largest pollard of those noted in Cudham occurred on the flint parish boundary bank adjacent to Leasons Wood. Its substantial crown growth, hanging towards the present pasture but away from existing woodland, indicates a date of last pollarding in c.1850, that is, in the period when Cudham Lodge Wood was cleared. With a girth of 268" its age is perhaps 482 years, with a date of planting in the early sixteenth century, although its growth may have been inhibited by an unfavourable situation, surrounded by other trees and with a poor resource base. Estate boundary pollards have continued to be cropped for poles into

53

PHOTO 1. POLLARDS ON THE NORTHERN EDGE OF GREAT MOLLOMS WOOD TQ454624

54

PHOTO 2.POLLARDS ON THE NORTHERN EDGE OF GREAT MOLLOMS WOOD TQ454624

the mid-twentieth century (pers. comm. Mr Hick, farmer, New Barn Farm). An analysis of overall age of the pollards in Cudham suggests their planting was in the early post-Medieval period. They indicate an attempt by landowners to mark permanence and longevity, particularly when used in conjunction with estate boundaries, appearing as a contradiction in a period of large-scale woodland clearance.

WOODLANDS FIELDWORK: THE FINDINGS
A general typology of the banks in Cudham is produced in fig. 7. When compared to the range of woodland earthworks shown in fig. 8, the Cudham banks appear dissimilar to woodland banks and more similar to Anglo-Saxon boundary banks. There were no ditches visible on the surface on either side of the banks, although they may have become filled in over time. Given that much of the banking is on steeply sloping ground and is associated with trackways, they may not necessarily have existed. The sectional diagram (fig. 9) illustrates that much of the banking is now covered in trees and underwood. The area enclosed by the banking was, at some point, converted to arable or pasture and the banks were used as a limited woodland resource, with hedgerows along each edge. Analysis of the age and species of the standards and coppices on the banking suggests that this was a post-Medieval phenomenon. Such woodland has aided the preservation of the banks from ploughing and erosion. The banks principally consist of flint boulders and clay soil and generally demarcate the division between the clay with flint and the chalk soils, thus potentially creating two different resource areas, although this is not exclusively the case.

Area 1
Fieldwork in this area consisted of inspections of Jewels Wood, of the trackway from the Biggin Hill Valley to the Roman road, and a detailed survey of the banks on the east facing slope of the valley near Skid Hill farm. The banked area was selected as a possible access point to a complex of woodlands on the clay with flint plateau, hinted at by the banking running across the slope rather than following the contours, as shown in photo 5. Analysis of the landscape presented in fig. 10 suggests that the banks may mark a divide between two crofts and their associated fields. The terrace on the eastern edge of the Eight Acre Horse Croft (place name derived from Old English *horh* meaning dirty, Wallenberg, 1934:530), with its commanding view down the Biggin Hill Valley, as shown in photo 3, suggests a strategic rather than purely agricultural use. It commands views of the valley not available from Biggin Hill itself, although the two places are intervisible. Alternatively, the creation of a flint and clay terraced area may represent an extension of the croft for a specific purpose, such as the storage of hay, although the area is somewhat large for this purpose.

Jewels Wood is an oak plantation with areas of hazel coppice and birch regeneration. Its eastern edge is framed by a line of beech standards, which are perhaps 200 years old. The road that skirts the wood runs within a hollow way. The western edge of the wood has a nineteenth century field boundary, inside of which is a 1m high flint bank, surmounted by a hawthorn hedgerow and layered ash grown out to standards, suggesting its earlier use as a shaw. This wood exhibits changing usage in the post-Medieval period, although the banking may be earlier.

Boundary bank

Examples: terrace at Skid Hill;
eastern edge of Homefield Spring

Parish boundary bank

Example: between Cudham
Lodge Wood and Leasons
Wood

Compartment

Flat top bank

Example: Biggin Hill airfield perimeter

Hollow Way

0   5   10m

Example: Snag Lane, edge of Great Molloms Wood

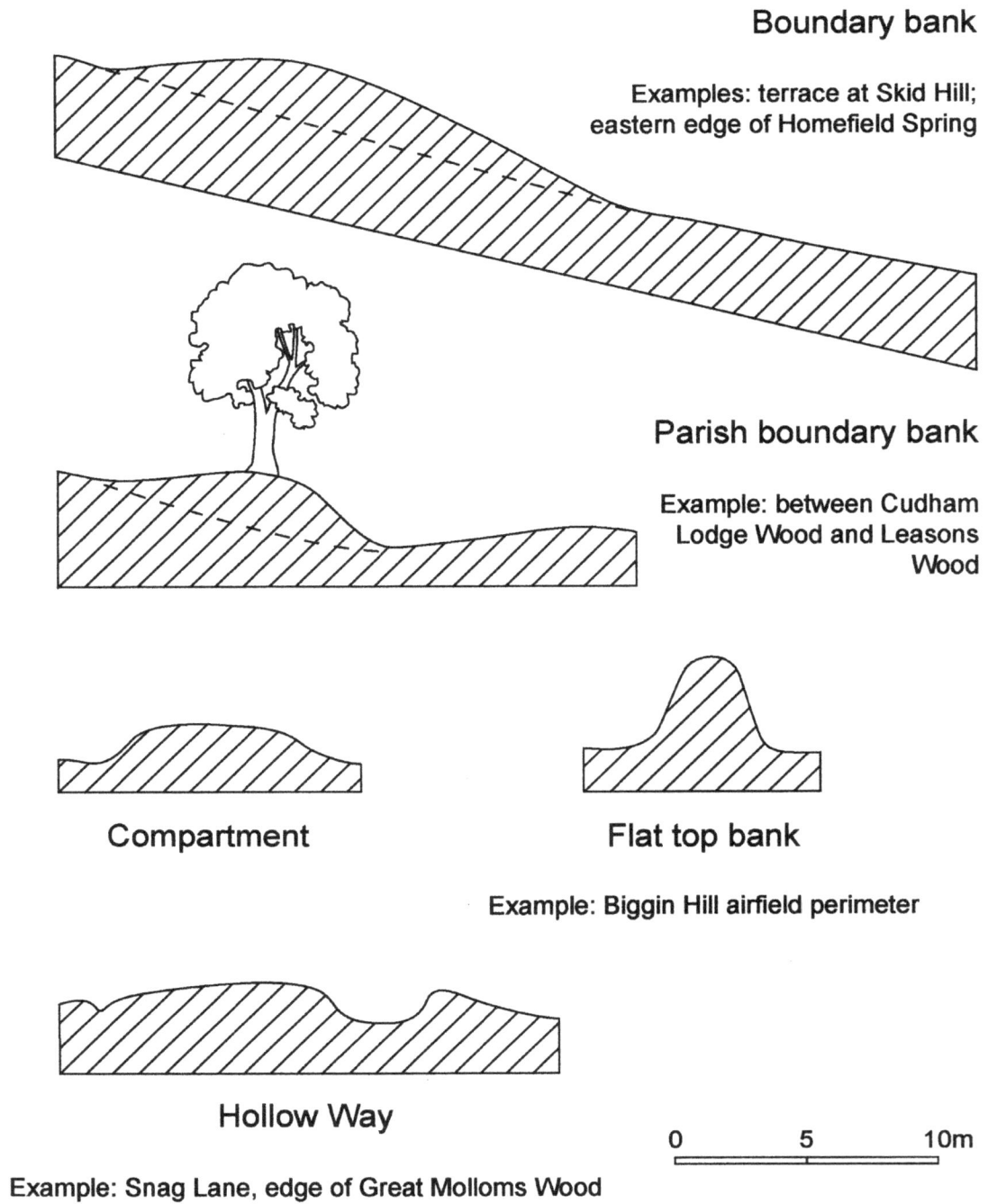

FIGURE 7. A TYPOLOGY OF BANKS IN CUDHAM

Woodland Earthworks (after Steane 1984)

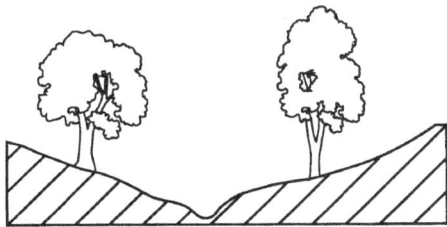

Drainage Grip

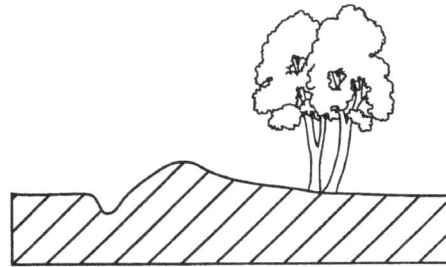

Wood Boundary Bank

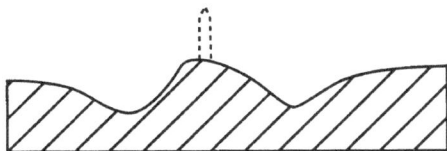

Medieval Park Pale

Coppice Bank

Saxon Boundary Banks (after Hoskins 1955)

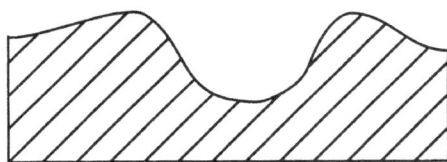

Estate Boundaries
Creating Hollow Way

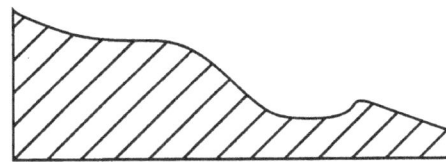

Estate Boundary on Slope
with Trackway

FIGURE 8. A TYPOLOGY OF WOODLAND EARTHWORKS

FIELD or WOOD

ROUGH/SHAW with coppice stools, possibly post medieval

TRACKWAY average width between hedges 3.6m

ROUGH/SHAW with coppice stools, possibly post medieval

18th/19th-century FIELD DITCH

FIELD or WOOD

LINE OF HEDGEROW
probably post medieval including
standards and layered plants grown out
to standards, particularly beech

FLINT BOULDER BANK

CLAY WITH FLINTS

CHALK

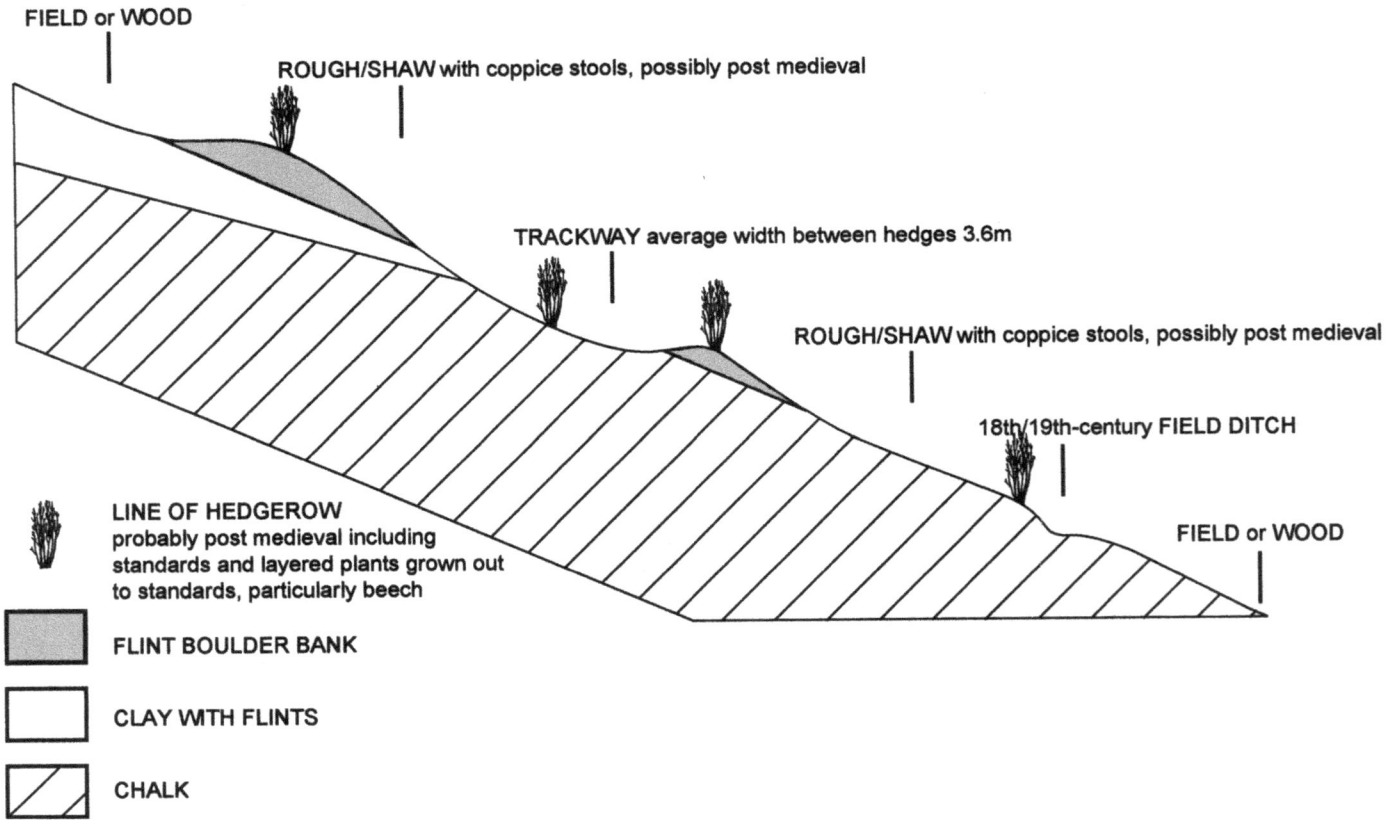

FIGURE 9. A SECTIONAL DIAGRAM THROUGH A BANK AND ASSOCIATED TRACKWAY

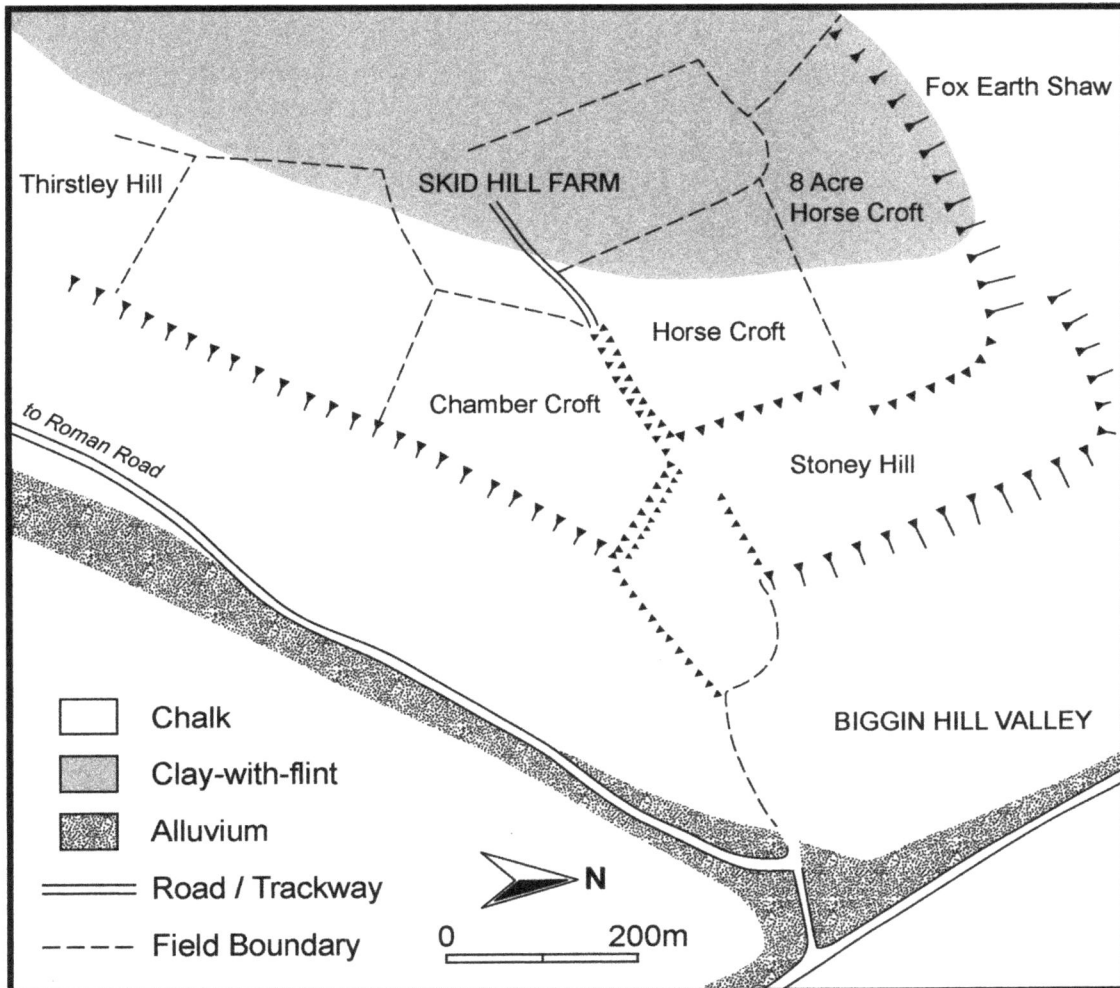

FIGURE 10. SKID HILL BANKS

PHOTO 3.SKID HILL FARM – EDGE OF TERRACE, LOOKING NORTH UP
THE BIGGIN HILL VALLEY TQ404603

The trackway from the western parish boundary to the Biggin Hill valley was walked in order to assess the junction of the Roman road, the track itself and the banking originating from the edge of Chamber Croft, as shown in photo 4. That they do meet up might suggest that the Roman road was used to delineate the boundary of the lands centred on the croft, particularly as the agger and adjacent ditches of the Roman road are still in evidence today, as shown in photos 6 and 7.

Area 2

In order to address the issue of the nature of Cudham Lodge Wood, the extant remnant of woodland, named Pimlico Wood, was examined from footpaths. The tree species here were mixed, with oak and sweet chestnut standards and discrete areas of hazel, oak, ash and sweet chestnut coppice stools of substantial size. The largest oak stool measured 285 cm x 235 cm, with an estimated age of 550 years. A sweet chestnut stool on the edge of the wood, in what was perhaps a hedgerow, measured 325 cm x 100 cm, with an estimated age of 600 years. Unusually, there was also a beech pollard within the wood (girth 367 cm, giving an estimated minimum age of 207 years). The accident of this wood's survival and the very mixed nature of the tree species suggest that it was a compartment within the larger wood, providing a range of wood resources for a single owner. However, there is no banking other than a 19th century field boundary associated with it. A late Medieval date of planting is suggested, perhaps in the fifteenth century.

Area 3

The sampled section of this area is shown in fig. 11. Pits located along the trackway to the north of Bombers Farm may be a source of flints for local buildings. The banking around Alder Haw is substantial on the track side, as shown in photo 8, but the western edge of the haw has been lost to ploughing, as shown in photo 9. The north-eastern corner of Shieling field is surmounted by a beech pollard of 515 cm girth (206"), with a minimum age estimated at 290 years.

The northernmost end of the track opens out into a valley, but the substantial banking returns eastwards, and is marked by a beech pollard (girth 492 cm/197", minimum age estimated at 277 years). The banking continues eastwards up a steep slope where it loses definition in Cudham Frith. The return corner was once marked by a large beech tree, of which only the decayed stump remains. It is therefore suggested that this banking represents an earlier edge of Cudham Frith and may be pre-Conquest in origin. As this is a homogenous complex of banking including the trackway, a pre-Conquest date of origin is suggested for all these features. The similarity in form between woodland boundary banks and enclosure banks, particularly those around the haw, highlights the problem of ascribing definitive functions to either.

Area 4

Great Molloms Wood is accessible from Snag Lane, the trackway that runs along its western edge. Snag Lane is a hollow way, with an average width of approximately 4m between its banks. The row of pollards that delineates the northern edge of this wood stands 13m in front of a 1m high flint bank. This is a rare example of a wood with an obviously changed boundary, created to accommodate the pollards in perhaps the late seventeenth century. The eastern edge of the wood also has a boundary bank delineating it. The wood is diagonally bisected by an avenue of beech standards, perhaps dating from the early nineteenth century. The southern edge of the wood has a shallow bank, 8m wide by .6m at its highest point, and is a rare example in Cudham of a woodland compartment bank.

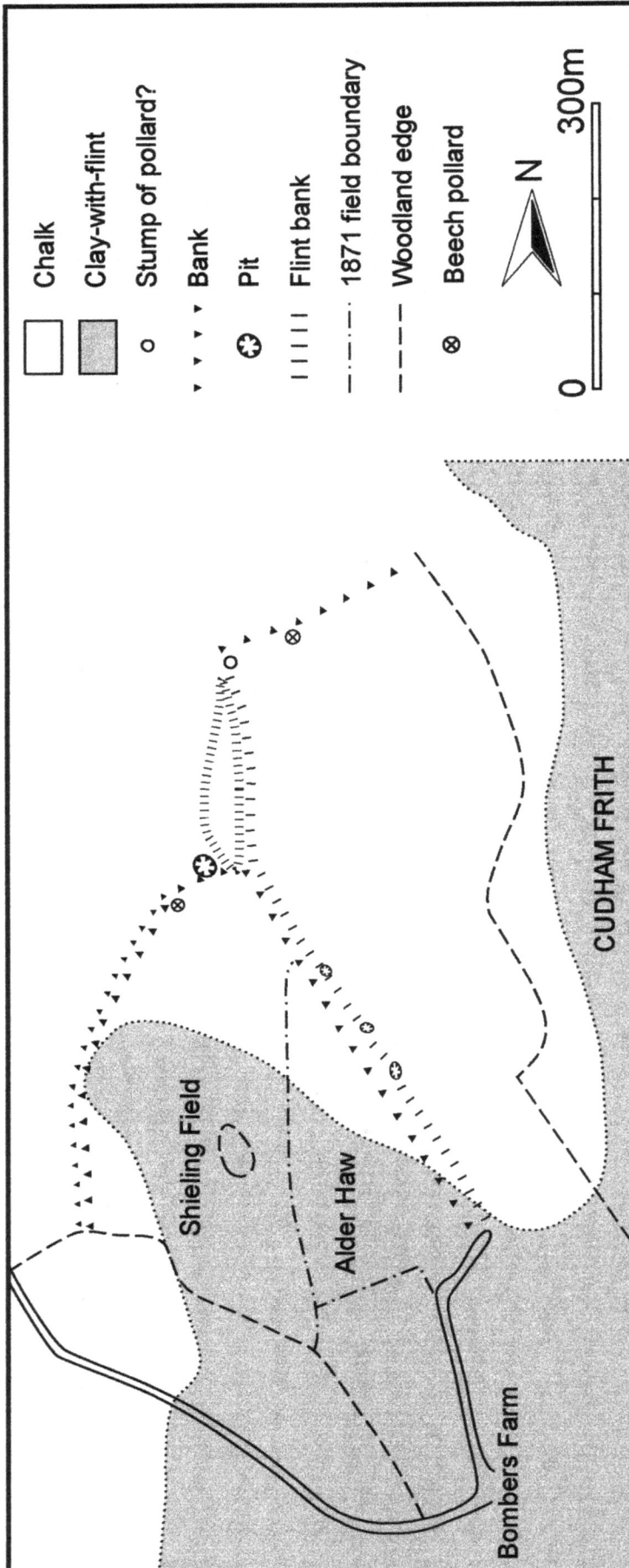

FIGURE 11. ALDER HAW AND SHIELING FIELD BANKS

Legend:
- Chalk
- Clay-with-flint
- Stump of pollard?
- Bank
- Pit
- Flint bank
- 1871 field boundary
- Woodland edge
- Beech pollard

N
0 ——— 300m

Shieling Field
Alder Haw
Bombers Farm
CUDHAM FRITH

63

PHOTO 4.CHAMBER CROFT AND PLOUGHED OUT BANKING FROM JERRY RIDDEN GROVE TQ406578

PHOTO 5. SKID HILL FARM EARTHWORKS FROM THE KESTON TO TATSFIELD ROAD
TQ411604

65

PHOTO 6. TRACKWAY FROM THE ROMAN ROAD TO BIGGIN HILL VALLEY TQ403595

PHOTO 7. DITCH BESIDE THE ROMAN ROAD TQ402594

PHOTO 8. TRACKWAY ON THE EASTERN EDGE OF ALDER HAW TQ448578

PHOTO 9. TRACKWAY TO THE WESTERN EDGE OF SHIELING FIELD TQ446578

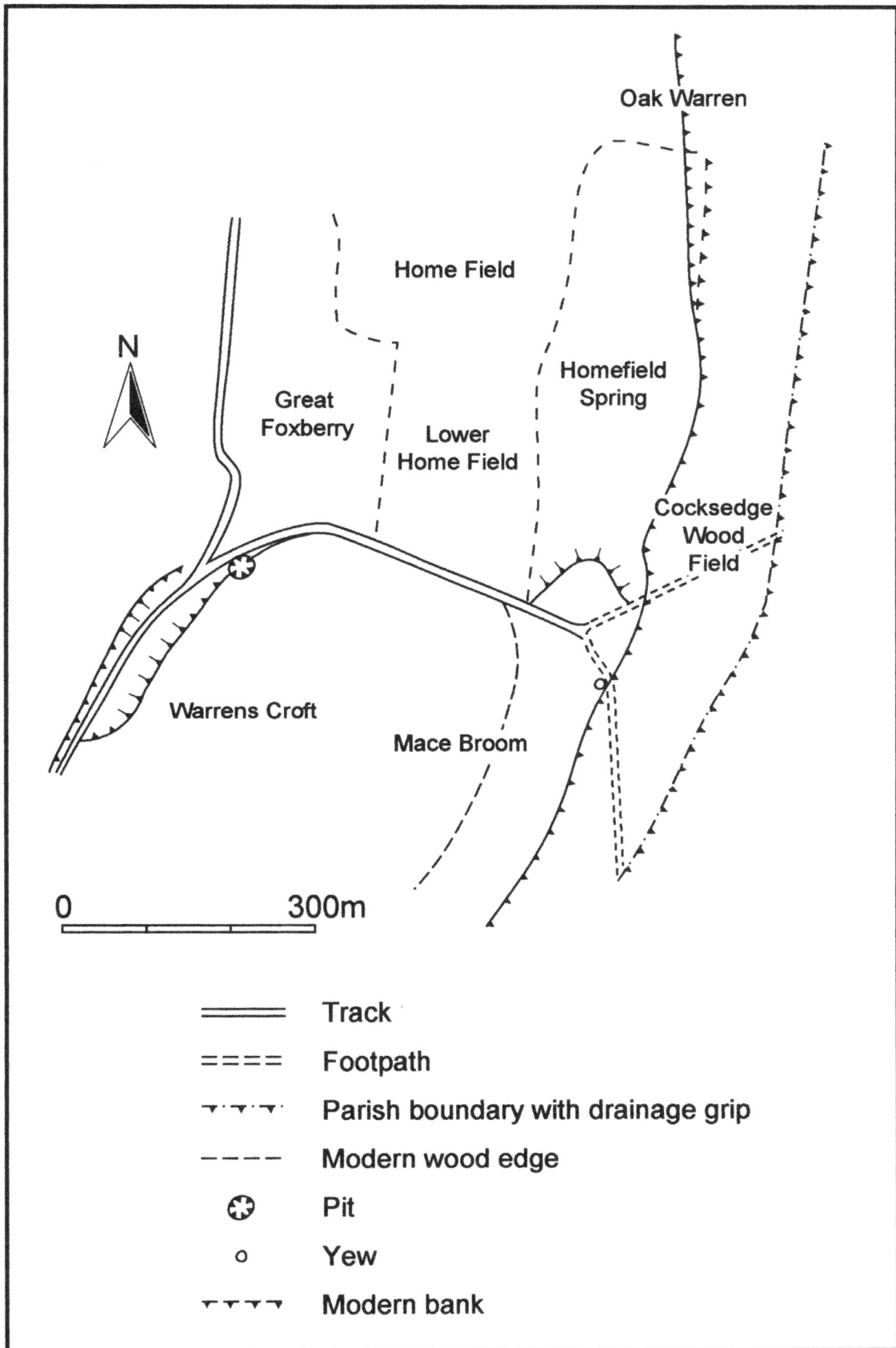

FIGURE 12. HOMEFIELD SPRING BANKS

The banking along the eastern edge of Homefield Spring is examined in detail in fig. 12. The north-eastern edge has been subsumed by a modern field bank (absent on the 1871 map), although this is identical in form to much earlier banks. The original line of this enclosure visibly continues to Little Molloms Wood, thus indicating that it predated the field now named Oak Warren. The tree species of ash and yew along the banking were consistent with those of a grown out hedgerow. A single yew tree, located at the intersection of the banking and the footpath, was aged at approximately 500 years.

Discrete tree communities of hornbeam, ash and oak coppice were identified within Homefield Spring, with other areas of birch regeneration. Compartments within this wood were not clearly defined and may have relied on hedgerows to delineate them. In its present form Homefield Spring appears to be a late Medieval coppice, although the banking may be much earlier.

Parish Boundary

The boundary was sampled in four locations. The objective was to determine whether it was intended as a notional boundary or as a physical barrier. At the lower edge of Cocksedge Wood Field it appears as a drainage grip. The eastern edge of Cudham Frith did not appear to have a boundary bank. This area has been encroached upon by modern housing and the line of this boundary has changed in the last two centuries, judged by comparisons of maps. The coincidence of the western boundary and the Roman road has already been noted (Area 1, Skid Hill Farm).

The boundary appears as a significantly large bank where it divides two woods, that is Cudham Lodge Wood and Leasons Wood in Downe. That the boundary retains a banked character running northwards is evident, although it has been much intercut by later features, such as banked hedgerows and flat top banks. The banking here supports the perception that in strategic places a clear distinction was made between woodlands, so that access to them was physically restricted. An explanation is therefore offered for the name Sow Wood, indicating that the banks were intended to prevent unlawful pannage by people from the neighbouring parish.

CONCLUSIONS

The data generated by the field surveys, place name evidence, maps and historical sources is presented in map form in figs. 13-15. This gives a general phasing and cannot be taken as definitive, due to the sampling nature of the research, or as precisely dated. Nevertheless, based on synthesis of the evidence, a chronological development of Cudham's landscape is discernible.

Current archaeological evidence shows little impact on the Downs by the Romans, nor indeed by earlier Iron Age communities, apart from that of the London-Lewes road and the trackways. The early Anglo-Saxon settlers to the north of the Downs probably made use of these trackways to reach woodland grazing in the leys on the lower slopes, and to reach summer sheep pastures on the clay with flint plateau. Discrete enclosures associated with hunting rights may also date to this period, as indicated in phase map 1.

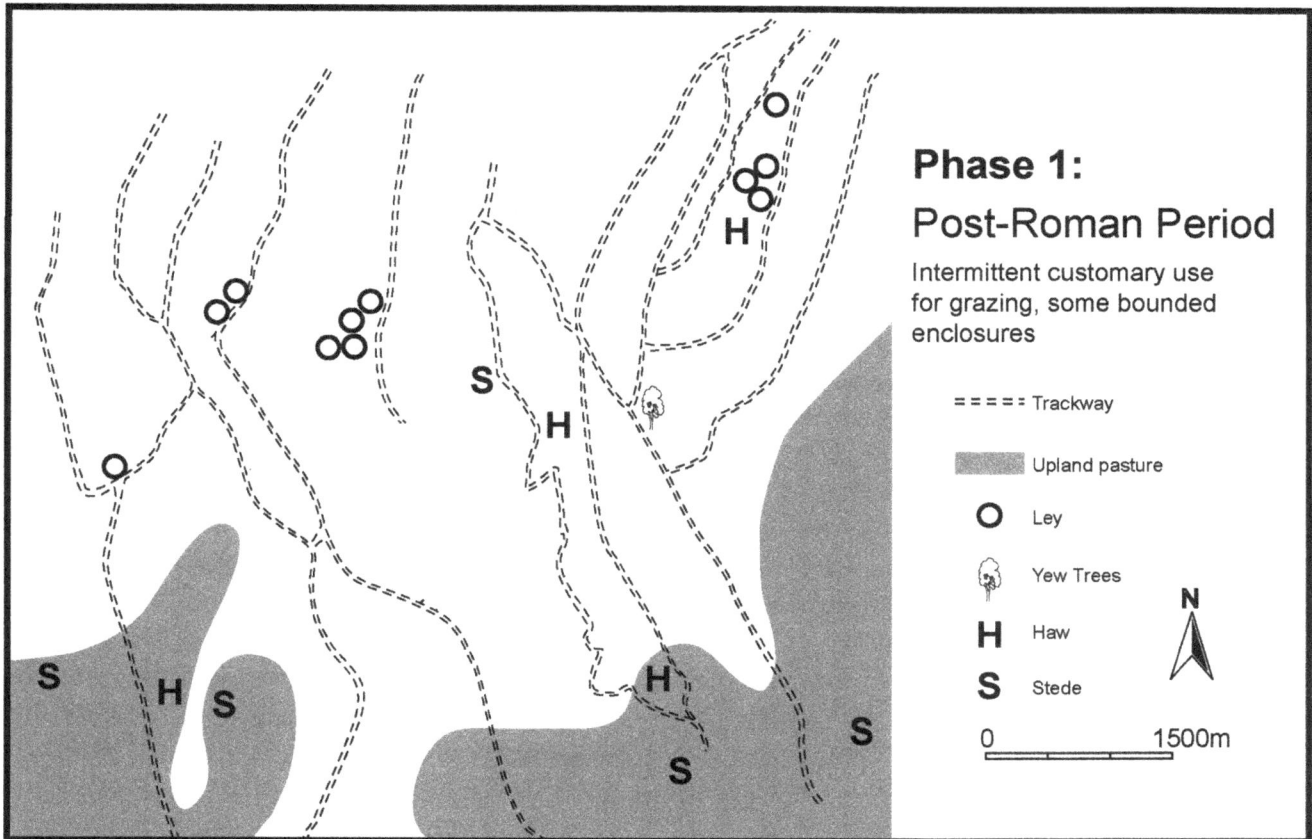

FIGURE 13. PHASE I OF LAND USE IN CUDHAM: THE POST ROMAN PERIOD

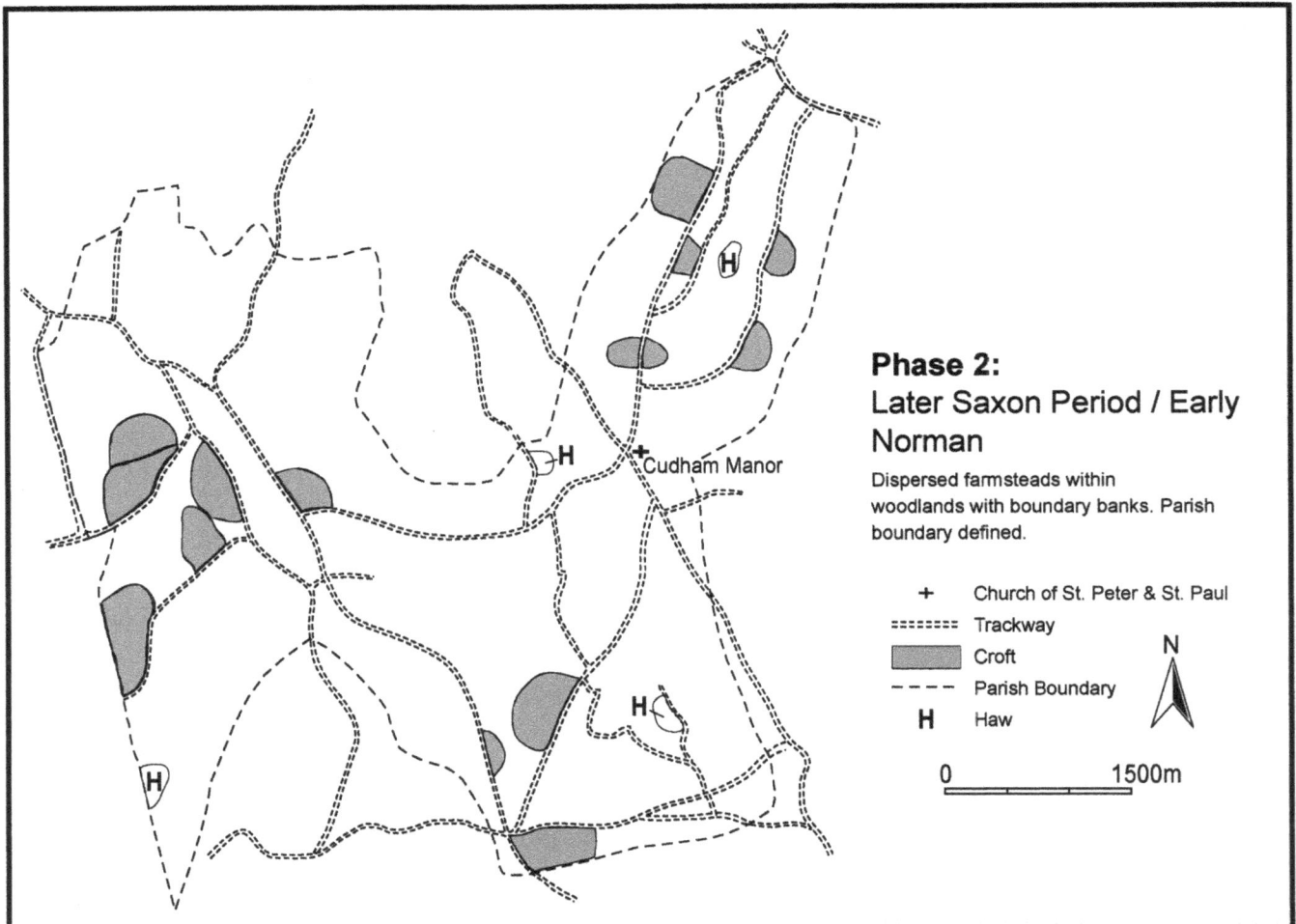

Phase 2:
Later Saxon Period / Early
Norman

Dispersed farmsteads within
woodlands with boundary banks. Parish
boundary defined.

+   Church of St. Peter & St. Paul
:::::::   Trackway
▨   Croft
- - -   Parish Boundary
H   Haw

N

0   1500m

FIGURE 14. PHASE II OF LAND USE IN CUDHAM: THE LATER SAXON/EARLY NORMAN
PERIOD

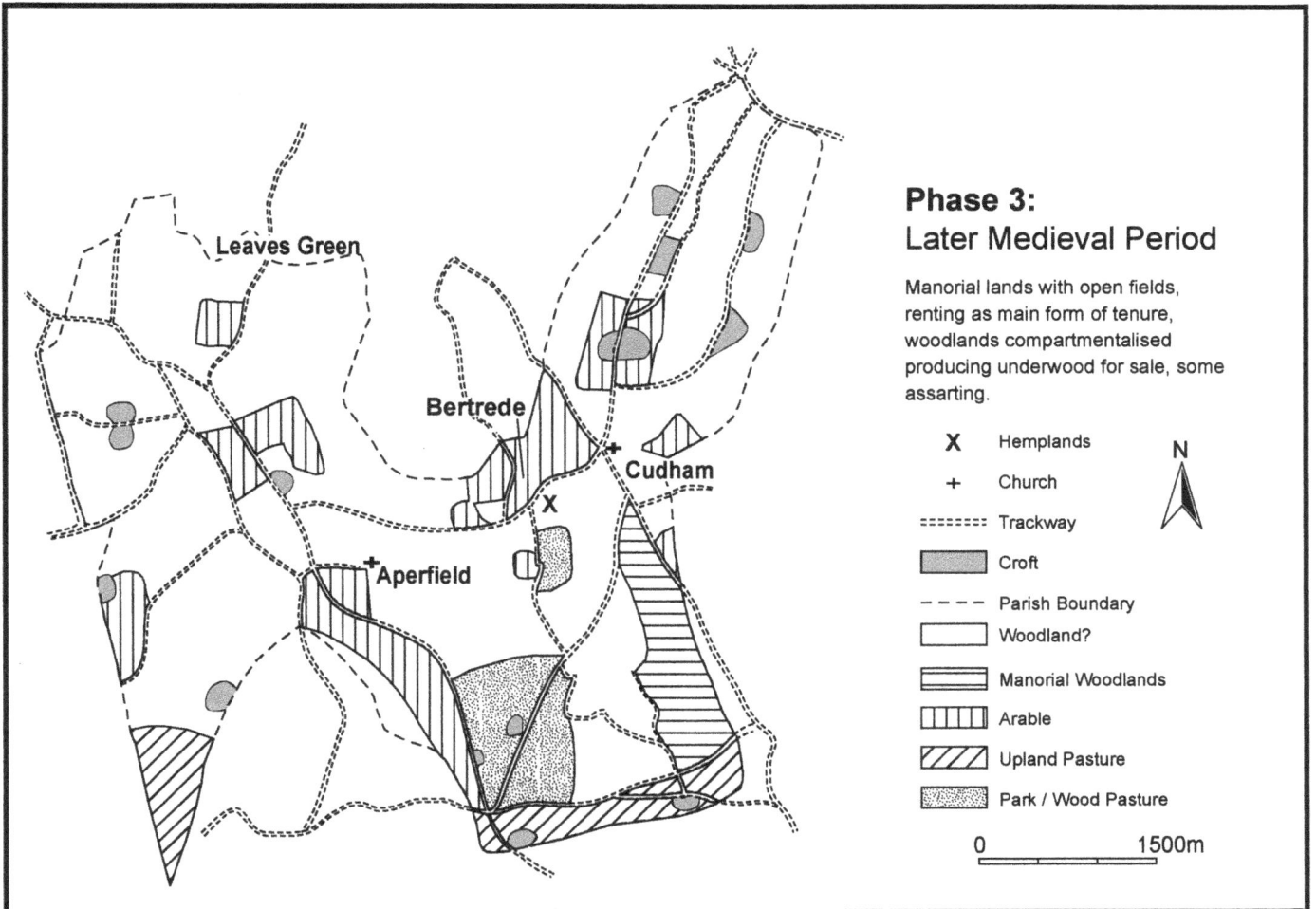

Phase 3:
Later Medieval Period

Manorial lands with open fields, renting as main form of tenure, woodlands compartmentalised producing underwood for sale, some assarting.

X	Hemplands
+	Church
========	Trackway
▨	Croft
- - - -	Parish Boundary
☐	Woodland?
▤	Manorial Woodlands
⊞	Arable
▨	Upland Pasture
░	Park / Wood Pasture

0 _____ 1500m

FIGURE 15. PHASE III OF LAND USE IN CUDHAM: THE LATER MEDIEVAL PERIOD

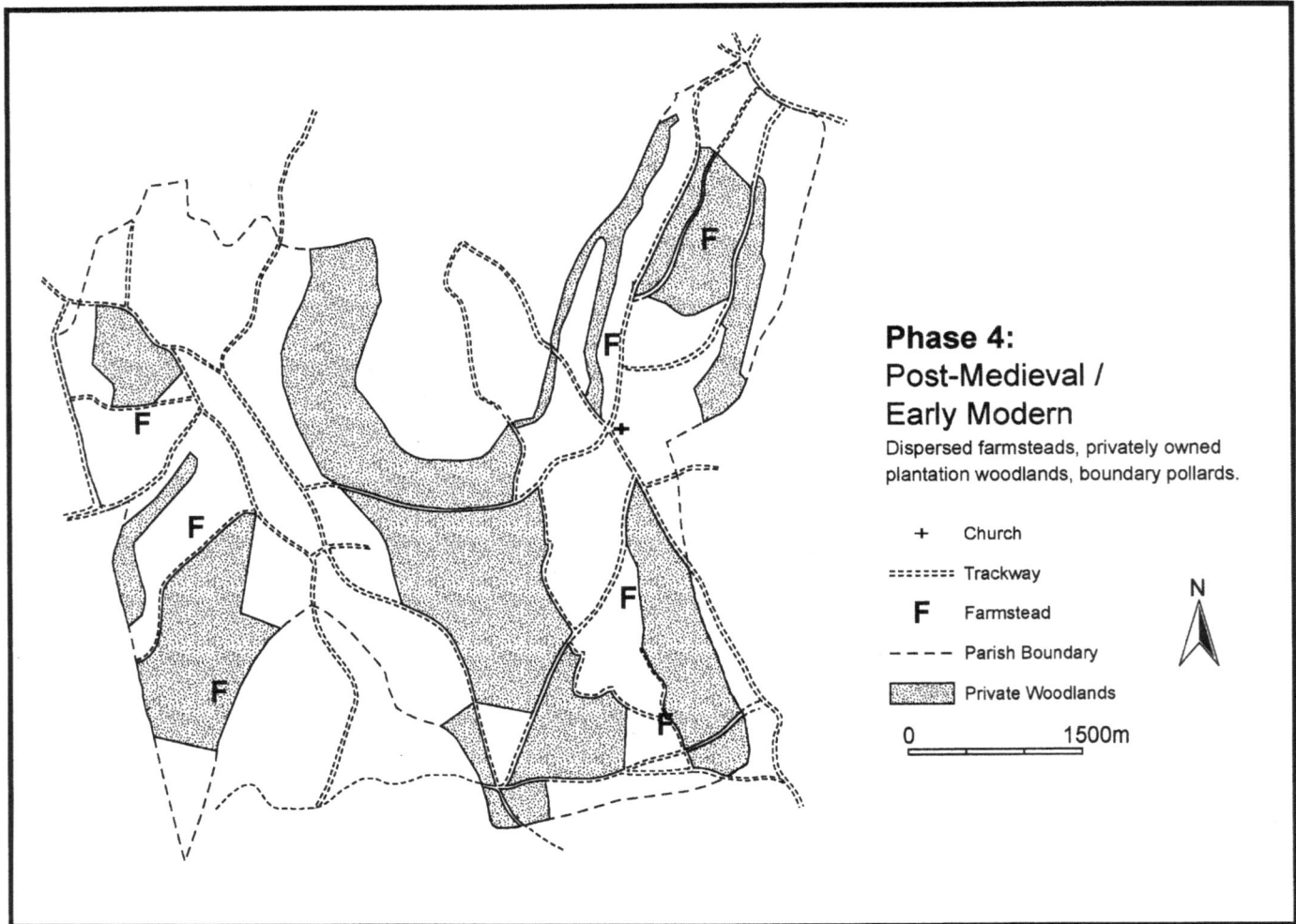

Phase 4:
Post-Medieval /
Early Modern
Dispersed farmsteads, privately owned
plantation woodlands, boundary pollards.

+   Church

::::::::   Trackway

F   Farmstead

- - - -   Parish Boundary

     Private Woodlands

0   1500m

N

FIGURE 16. PHASE IV OF LAND USE IN CUDHAM: THE POST-MEDIEVAL/EARLY MODERN
PERIOD

In the second phase (map 2), there is evidence for settlement on the plateau, with dispersed landholdings and some communal features such as the mills and burial in the churchyard, associated with a manorial holding in Cudham. Woodland appears as the dominant feature of the landscape. In the later Medieval period, outlined in phase map 3, the woodlands may have become compartmentalised, used to produce underwood and billets for sale elsewhere, within a mixed agricultural economy with a limited open field system under the aegis of the manors, but with the dispersed, rent paying farmsteaders still in evidence within the woodlands. The post-Medieval period, outlined in phase 4, was one where woodlands were again dominant, being re-planted as part of the estates of local landowners, although the isolated farmsteads continued in use.

The research questions that this study in woodland archaeology in Cudham sought to address were prompted by an anomaly between two documentary sources. The Domesday Book reference implied extensive ploughlands, with 10 ploughs, whilst the early nineteenth century reference implied extensive woodlands. In the light of the subsequent research programme discussed here, these might now be reconsidered.

It is suggested that Cudham is an anomaly by virtue of its size. Referring to the comparison of Domesday references discussed earlier, the density of ploughs per head of population is not abnormal. The place-name evidence, based on the distribution of crofts as indicative of settlement activity, indicates a much dispersed pattern of living and farming that militated against nucleation and the sharing of resources. The location of crofts on the clay with flint plateau, adjacent to trackways fixed in the landscape by the transhumance of stock from manors to the north of the Downs, perhaps indicates that the chalk valleys and the rest of the plateau were wooded. Nevertheless, the crofts were sited to take advantage of the range of soil types and resources available.

The extensive woodlands noted in the later reference probably refer to what became known as Cudham Lodge Wood. This was probably a post-Medieval amalgamation of woodland compartments that had produced surplus underwood for sale in market economy. It is significant that the instances of dominant settlements at Aperdrefeld and Bertrede are associated with open fields that do not encroach on the main woodland areas. If anything the open fields themselves are marginal. However, such is the scale of the parish that there was room to accommodate these changes without impinging on the main economic resource. The extent to which the documentary and location evidence for Aperdrefeld, Bertrede and Cudham represents settlement nucleation rather ribbon development along major routeways remains conjectural.

Little trace has been found of the other forms of woodland. Documentary sources note the existence of parks but no archaeological remains of them, such as a park pale, could be identified. Place-name evidence might suggest that they became subsumed in Cudham Lodge Wood. Common woods were probably located at Berry's Green, Leaves Green and Horn's Green, on the periphery of the central woodland plateau. Instances of wood pasture are rare, indicating perhaps that stock grazing was not central to the agricultural regime in the later Medieval period. The pollarded beeches relate to a redefinition of post-Medieval boundaries and are sited on banks that are much earlier.

Whilst there are few examples of coppice in the parish, those that do exist are probably later and post-Medieval in origin, for example Homefield Spring. Nevertheless, coppicing is evident in the ecofactual remains, as shown in photos 10 and 11, particularly in Cudham Frith, which is a defined area of clearly pre-Conquest origin, if not pre-Roman. The

PHOTO 10.BEECH COPPICE STOOLS IN CUDHAM FRITH TQ452581

PHOTO 11.BEECH COPPICE STOOL IN CUDHAM FRITH TQ452581

designation of a specific area for the production of woodland products, that is the billets and shingles from around Skid Hill, indicates surplus production for a market economy. This activity is perhaps contemporary with the mid fourteenth century reference to the neighbouring manor of Farleigh.

The incidence of *mal* lands again stresses the influence of the market economy, whereby it had become economic to manage the woodlands for surplus production, rather than converting them to arable. The incidence of assarting is limited to area 4, underlining the strength of the woodland economy within the parish. In summation, the landscape of the parish of Cudham appears to have been organised as a specialist regime producing a range of woodland products in London's hinterland in the later Medieval period, a role that continued into the nineteenth century.

As the phased maps show, it has only been possible to indicate some very broad outlines of change within the parish. The methodology adopted for this research project necessitated the development of in-depth local knowledge and an understanding of woodland forms and species. A synthesis of all of the evidence, made without allowing hegemony to any particular form, allows the following analysis to be made. The extant earthwork banking in the parish appears to relate to the earliest phases of settlement of the North Downs, although they were used specifically as woodland boundaries at a later date. The profiles of the banking alone, given that this may be the same regardless of date of origin, does not indicate their initial purpose. The distribution of and linkages between the banks suggest the outlines of small estates, as delineated perhaps by groups of Anglo-Saxon settlers in the period c. AD500-900.

The patterns that these people imposed on the landscape have endured, in a fragmented form, into the twentyfirst century. This landscape, unique within the boundaries of Greater London, is, however, threatened by piecemeal encroachment. It is imperative, therefore, that archaeological fieldwork is carried out in the parish in the near future. A minimum requirement would be a programme of fieldwalking, targeting initially the early Medieval fields identified in this project, together with a full survey of the extant banking and ecofactual remains. From this base might be established a fuller understanding of the role that this anomalous, but unique, tract of the North Downs has played in London's past.

BIBLIOGRAPHY

Aston, M. 1985. *Interpreting the landscape*. London: B.T.Batsford.

Bannister, N. 1996. *Woodland Archaeology in Surrey*. Kingston upon Thames: Surrey County Council Planning Dept.

Bird, D.G. 1987. The Romano-British period in Surrey. In Bird, J. and Bird, D.G. (eds), *The Archaeology of Surrey to 1540*: 165-196. Guildford: Surrey Archaeological Society.

Blair, J. 1991. *Early Medieval Surrey*. Stroud: Alan Sutton Publishing and Surrey Archaeological Society.

Bolton, J.L. 1980. *The English Medieval Economy 1150-1500*. London: Dent Everymans.

Boys, J. 1796. *General view of the agriculture of the county of Kent*. London: G. Nicol.

Brandon, P and Short, B. 1990. *The south-east from AD1000*. Harlow: Longman Group.

Burton, R.M. 1983. *The flora of the London area*. London: London Natural History Society.

Campbell, B., Galloway, J and Murphy, M. 1992. Rural Land-use in the Metropolitan Hinterland, 1270-1339: the evidence of Inquisitiones Post Mortem. *Agricultural History Review*, **40.1**:1-22.

Campbell, E. 1962. Kent. In Darby, H.C. and Campbell, E. (eds), *The Domesday geography of south-east England*: 483-562. Cambridge: Cambridge University Press.

Cantor, L. 1982. *The English Medieval landscape*. London: Croom Helm.

Cater, J. and Jones, T. 1989. *Social Geography*. London: Edward Arnold.

Clarke, A.F. 1982. The Neolithic of Kent: a review. In Leach, P.E.(ed) *The archaeology of Kent to AD1500*. Council of British Archaeology Research Report 48. London: C.B.A.

Clarke, H. 1984. *The Archaeology of Medieval England*. London: British Museum Publications.

Coles, J.M. 1978. The Somerset Levels: a concave landscape. In Bowen, H.C and Fowler, P.J. (eds) *Early Land Allotment in the British Isles*: 147-8. BAR (British Series) 48.

Cotton, J. 1995. Flint implements from the North Downs at Biggin Hill. *Kent Archaeological Review* **121**: 2-4.

Crozier, B. and Philp, B. 1985. *The archaeology of the Bromley area*. Kent Archaeological Rescue Unit.

Cunliffe, B. 1982. Social and economic development in Kent in the pre-Roman Iron-Age. In Leach, P.E. ed) *The archaeology of Kent to AD1500*. Council of British Archaeology Research Report 48. London: C.B.A.

Cunliffe, B. 1991. *Iron-Age communities in Britain*. London: Routledge.

Daniels, S. 1988. The political iconography of woodland in later Georgian England. In Cosgrove, D. and Daniels, S. *The iconography of landscape*: 43-80. Cambridge: Cambridge University Press.

Darby, H.C. 1951. *The Clearing of the English Woodlands*. Geography 36: 71-83

Dimbleby, G.W. 1970. Report on pollen analysis. In Piercy Fox, N. Caesar's Camp, Keston. *Archaeologia Cantiana* **84**: 185-199.

Domesday Book. See Morris, J. (1983)

Dyer, C. 1986. English Peasant Buildings in the Later Middle Ages (1200-1500). *Medieval Archaeology* **30**: 19-45.

Everitt, A. 1986. *Continuity and Colonisation: the evolution of Kentish settlement*. Leicester: University Press.

Evison, V. 1965. *The Fifth century invasions south of the Thames*. London: The Athlone Press, University of London.

Evison, V. 1987. *Dover: Buckland Anglo-Saxon cemetery*. London: Historic Buildings and Monuments Commission.

Field, J. 1993. *A History of English field-names*. London: Longman.

Flinders-Petrie, W.M. 1880. Notes on Kentish earthworks. *Archaeologia Cantiana* **13**: 1-15.

Forestry Authority. 1994. *Estimating the age of large trees in Britain*. Research Information Note 250. Farnham: The Forestry Authority.

Gander, M. n.d. *St. Peter and St. Paul, Cudham: analysis of the church restoration*. Unpublished.

Gardiner, M. 1984. Saxon settlement and land division in the Western Weald. *Surrey Archaeological Collections* **122**: 75-96.

Gelling, M. 1993. *Place-names in the landscape*. Paperback edition. London: J.M.Dent.

Gold, M. 1984. A history of nature. In Massey, D and Allen, J. (eds) *Geography Matters!* 12-33. Cambridge: Cambridge University Press with The Open University.

Gomme, G.L. 1898. Cudham 1804. *English Topography pt.VI*. The Gentleman's Magazine Library. London: Eliot Stock.

Hasted, E. 1801. *The history and topographical survey of the county of Kent*. 2nd edition vol.2 EP Publishers and Kent County Library 1972 facsimile of the1801 edition.

Hawkes, S.C. 1973. The dating and social significance of the burials in the Polhill Cemetery. In Philp, B. (ed) *Excavations in West Kent 1960-1970*. Dover.

Hayes, A.1994. *Indicative Forestry and Woodland Strategy*. Bromley: Bromley Planning Department.

Hayes, A. 1995. *Hedgerows in Bromley*. Bromley: Bromley Planning Department.

Hewlett, G. 1973. Reconstructing a historical landscape from field and documentary evidence: Otford in Kent. *Agricultural History Review* **21**: 94-110.

Hewlett, G. 1980. Stages in the settlement of a downland parish: a study of the hedges of Chelsham. *Surrey Archaeological Collections* **72**: 91-96.

Hodges, H. 1989. *Artifacts*. London: Duckworth.

Hooke, D. 1989. Pre-Conquest Woodland: its Distribution and Usage. *Agricultural History Review* **37.II**: 113-129.

Hoskins, W.G. 1955. *The Making of the English Landscape*. Harmondsworth: Penguin Pubs.

Johnson, M. 1996. *An Archaeology of Capitalism*. Oxford: Blackwell Pubs.

Kinnibrugh, G. 1976. A history of Cudham. *Cudham Parish News*. January/February edition: 7-11

Megaw, J.V.S. and Simpson, D.D.A. 1979. *Introduction to British Prehistory*. Leicester: Leicester University Press.

Meredith, A. 1984. *Report on the Yew trees in the churchyard of St.Peter and St.Paul, Cudham*. Unpublished notes.

Miles, D. and Branigan, K. 1986. *The economies of Romano-British villas*. Sheffield: J.R. Collis.

Millett, M. 1992. *The Romanization of Britain*. Cambridge: Cambridge University Press.

Mills, A.D. 1991. *Dictionary of English Place Names*. Oxford: University Press.

Milne, G. 1995. *Roman London*. London: B.T.Batsford/English Heritage.

Mitchell, A. 1978. *Trees of Britain and Northern Europe*. 2nd edition London: Collins.

Mitchell, A. 1994. Letter. *Surrey Historic Landscape Studies Newsletter* **5**: 5.

Morgan, R.A. 1988 *Tree ring studies of wood used in the Neolithic and Bronze Age trackways from the Somerset Levels*. BAR (British Series) 184.

Morris, J.(ed). 1983. *The Domesday Book*. Chichester: Phillimore Press.

Needham, S. 1987. The Bronze Age. In Bird, J. and Bird, D.G. (eds) *The Archaeology of Surrey to 1540*. 97-137. Guildford: Surrey Archaeological Society.

Nelson, J. 1982. *Grandfather's Biggin Hill*. Westerham: John Nelson

Ordnance Survey. *1871 Kent Sheet XXI*. Scale 6" to 1 mile

Ordnance Survey. 1989. *Pathfinder map no.1192, Orpington.* Scale 1:25000

Ordnance Survey. 1989. *Pathfinder map no.1208, Sevenoaks.* Scale 1:25000

Orpington and District Archaeological Society. 1993a. *The Upper Cray Valley 4000-700BC.* Orpington: ODAS.

Orpington and District Archaeological Society. 1993b. *The Upper Cray Valley 700BC-AD410.* Orpington: ODAS Orpington and District Archaeological Society.

Patch, D. 1994. Letter. *Surrey Historic Landscape Studies Newsletter* **5**: 5.

Pearman, R.G. n.d. *The early history of Cudham and its church.* Orpington: Orpington History and Record Society.

Pedersen, L. 1995. 7000 years of fishing: stationery structures in the Mesolithic and afterwards. In Fischer, A. (ed). *Man and Sea in the Mesolithic.* 75-86. Oxford: Oxbow Books.

Peterken, G.1993. *Woodland Conservation and Management.* 2nd edition. London: Chapman and Hall.

Philp, B. (ed.) 1973. *Excavations in West Kent 1960-1970.* Dover: Kent Archaeological Rescue Unit.

Poulton, R. 1987. Saxon Surrey. In Bird, J. and Bird, D.G. (eds.) *The Archaeology of Surrey to 1540.* 197-222. Guildford: Surrey Archaeological Society.

Pryor, F. 1991. *Flag Fen.* London: B.T.Batsford/English Heritage.

Rackham, O 1977 Neolithic woodland management in the Somerset Levels: Garvin's, Walton Heath and Rowland's Tracks. *Somerset Levels Papers* **3**: 65-71

Rackham, O. 1986. *The Woods of South-East Essex.* Rochford: Rochford District Council.

Rackham, O. 1995a. *Trees and Woodland in the British Landscape.* London: Weidenfeld and Nicolson.

Rackham, O. 1995b. *The history of the countryside.* London: Weidenfeld and Nicolson.

Reynolds, A. 1998. Executions and hard Anglo-Saxon justice. *British Archaeology* **31**: 8-9.

Roach Smith, C. 1863. Note. *Archaeologia Cantiana* **5**: 331.

Roden, D. 1968. Woodland and its management in the Medieval Chilterns. *Forestry-The Journal of the Society of Foresters of Great Britain* **41**: 59-71.

Saaler, M. 1996. The Manor of Farleigh: the evidence for economic changes during the 14th century. *Surrey Archaeological Collections* **83**: 57-71.

Schama, S. 1995. *Landscape and Memory.* London: Fontana Press.

Sheldon, H., Corti, G., Green, D. and Tyers, P. 1993. The distribution of villas in Kent, Surrey and Sussex. *London Archaeologist* **7.2**: 40-5.

Stamper, P. 1983. The Medieval forest of Pamber, Hampshire. *Landscape History* **5**: 41-52.

Steane, J.1984. *The Archaeology of Medieval England and Wales*. London: Guild Publishing.

Steinman, G.S. 1851. *Some account of the manor of Apuldrefield in the parish of Cudham, Kent*. London: J.B. Nichols and Son.

Taylor, C. 1974. *Fieldwork in Medieval Archaeology*. London: B.T.Batsford.

Taylor, C. 1979. *The roads and tracks of Britain*. London: J.M.Dent.

Tester, P. 1969. An Anglo-Saxon cemetery at Orpington. *Archaeologia Cantiana* **83**: 125-50.

Thorne, J. 1876. *Handbook of the Environs of London*. 1983 facsimile edition Godfrey Cave Associates.

Turner, D.J. 1980. The North Downs Trackway. *Surrey Archaeological Collections* **72**: 1-12.

Turner, D.J. 1987. Archaeology of Surrey 1066 to 1540. In Bird, J. and Bird, D.G. (eds). *The Archaeology of Surrey to 1540* 223-261. Guildford: Surrey Archaeological Society.

Victoria County History. 1908. *Kent*. London: Archibald Constable.

Victoria County History. 1905. *Surrey*. London: Archibald Constable.

Wallenberg, J.K. 1931. *The place-names of Kent*. Uppsala: Appelbergs Boktryckeriaktiebolag.

Whitelock, D. 1965. *The Beginnings of English Society*. Revised edition. Harmondsworth; Penguin.

Williamson, T. and Bellamy, L. 1987. *Property and Landscape*. London: George Philip.

Williamson, T. 1988. Explaining Regional Landscapes: woodland and champion in Southern and Eastern England. *Landscape History* **10**: 5-13.

Witney, K.P. 1990. The Woodland Economy of Kent 1066-1348. *Agricultural History Review* **38.1**: 20-39.

Witney, K.P. 1987. The period of Mercian rule in Kent and a charter of AD811. *Archaeologia Cantiana* **104**: 87-113.

SUE HARRINGTON

APPENDIX 1 – THE TREE RECORDING SHEET

Site code   Sheet no.   Recorded by   Date

Grid ref.	Species	Form	Location	Soil	Crown	Environment	Comments	Girth at 1.5m	Calculated age

APPENDIX 2 - NAMES OF FIELDS IN THE MEDIEVAL CUDHAM MANORS, from contemporary documentary sources, paraphrasing interpretations of their meanings provided by Paul Cullen (pers. comm.) with direct quotations in inverted commas. My comments from field notes and additional queries are in italics.

Sequence of information:
Field name; date of document; manor holding this field; size in acres at that time; Tithe Apportionment (TA) number eg {211}

Werland; 1247; Apuldrefield; 10 acres; unknown
OE **land** 'land'. The first element is ambiguous. Formal possibilities include OE **wer, wær** 'weir, river-dam' and OE **wer(e)** '?guard, ?look-out'. *Tentatively associated with Woollards Hill {1042}, see main text.*

Northberden; 1360; unknown; unknown; TA unknown;
Southberden; 1360; unknown; unknown; unknown;
Affixes are north and south. *Berden is best regarded as obscure. Den is probably either OE **denu** 'long two-sided valley' or **denn** 'woodland pasture'. The first element has many possibilities, including OE **bere** 'barley', **bæ:r** 'bare, without vegetation' and **by:re** 'byre, cowshed', also could refer to a personal name. *Could these names also relate to the manor of Bertrede that was extant in this period?*

Mede; 1360; unknown; unknown; TA {1134}?
Meadow. May survive into the TA as the Mead. *This is a large field opposite Hostye Farm, see maps case study fig. 6 in main text.*

Thornfield; 1360; unknown; unknown; TA {1003} Thornfield Shaw, {1002} Lower Thornfield, {1001} Upper Thornfield.
OE **þorn** 'thorn-tree' + **feld** 'open land'. *Fields lying south of Cudham Hall and east of Cudham Lane.*

Brodefeld ; 1371, 1386; Apuldrefield; 50 acres; TA {870} Bradfield
OE **brād** 'broad' + **feld**. *Large field adjacent to Kemp Hill {866}.*

Schidden; 1371; Apuldrefield; unknown; uncertain
This may be a two element compound, with the second element **denu** or **denn** (see below). Wallenburg connects it to OE **scīd** 'thin slip of wood, shingle or billet' although the connection to Skid Hill may be tenuous. The precise sense of the word in place-names is variable. Possibly Schidden survives as TAs {254} Sheetings, {374} Sheetings Shaw, {368} First Sheetings and {373} Further Sheetings. *These fields are in a cluster on the east slope of the Biggin Hill valley opposite to Skid Hill and in proximity to Tanner's Bottom {258}, another, more modern, name also suggesting the use of oak products in the vicinity.*

Blenchfelde or **Glench**; 1371, 1386; Apuldrefield; 14 acres; TA {127} Great Glench, {125} Little Glench.
OE **feld**, otherwise no suggestible etymology. *Two fields adjacent to the main routeway through the Downs and on the trackway leading from the Biggin Hill valley to the Roman road/parish and county boundary, on alluvial soils.*

Plechfelde; 1371; Apuldrefield; 24 acres; unknown
OE **feld**, otherwise no suggestible etymology.

Chersebenefeld/Chersebemfeld; 1371; Apuldrefield; unknown; unknown
OE **ciris-bēam** 'cherry-tree' + **feld**.

Helde; 1386; Bertrede; 8 acres; uncertain

OE **helde** 'slope'. 'This name may well survive as Hell field {218], Hell field shaw {217}, Hell field Stock {214}, Hell field Stock shaw {216}. Such a development of **helde** is common.' *These four fields form a coherent block up the eastern slope of the Biggin Hill valley to the plateau and are located precisely below the hamlet named Biggin Hill on the 1871 OS map. Together they total 26 acres. Hell field {218} is 8 acres and lies at the top of the slope abutting the road.*

Nicholiers croft/Nichcoliers croft; 1386; Bertrede; 2 acres; uncertain
OE **croft** 'small enclosed plot'. 'This name is most satisfactorily explained as "Nick [i.e. Nicholas] Colliers croft" which suggests a possible connection with the TA name Colliers Lane Stock {211}, seemingly containing the same surname (from ME coliere 'charcoal maker or seller.' *The plot TA {211} completes the tranche of land on the eastern slope of the Biggin Hill valley discussed above and abuts the main trackway, now known as Oaklands Lane. {211} is much larger than Nicholiers croft at 14 acres, however.*

Hardem croft; 1386; Bertrede; 2 acres; unknown
OE **croft**. 'The Hardem component is a mystery'.

Adlene croft; 1386; Bertrede; 3 acres; unknown
OE **croft.** 'The first element is possibly the feminine personal name *Adeline* (from OG Adelina, a pet-form of Adelhaid), which is found as a surname in 13th century Kent'.

Stite croft; 1386; Bertrede; 3 acres; unknown
OE **croft**. No interpretation suggested.

Sparwhel; 1386; Bertrede; 2 acres; unknown
OE **spearwa** ' sparrow' fits the first element. 'The second element appears to be OE **hyll** 'hill' (with Kentish *e* for *y*), though **helde** with loss of *d* is a perfectly possible alternative.'

Cokkes croft; 1386; Bertrede; 3 acres; unknown
OE **croft**. 'The first element is most likely the surname *Cock*'.

Colewynes croft; 1386; Bertrede; 2 acres; unknown
OE **croft**. ' The first element looks like a surname … The OE masculine personal name *Colwine* is on record and may well have survived into the ME period'.

Herboun; 1386; Bertrede; 12 acres; unknown
No suggestible meaning.

Netherstrenely, Overstrenely; 1386; 9 acres, 8 acres; Bertrede; unknown
'The affixes are OE **neoðera** 'nether, lower' and **uferra** 'upper, higher'. The generic element looks like **lēah,** the specific is problematic.

Combelond; 1440; Apuldrefield; unknown; uncertain
OE **land**. 'OE cumb 'three-sided valley' is formally ideal … although …an alternative first element is OE **camb** 'comb, crest, ridge" *A connection to Cooper Coomb {942} is possible, although the location of this field, adjacent to the road through Berry's Green, favours neither explanation.*

Rodeland; 1440; Apuldrefield; unknown; uncertain
OE **land**. 'Plausible candidates for the first element are OE **rōd** 'rood, measure of lane', the indistinguishable OE **rōd** 'rood, cross' (perhaps with reference to land whose profits are used to maintain church furniture), and OE ***rodu** 'clearing'… A connection to TA Ridlands {796} looks possible … and might thus argue in favour of ***rodu**'. *Ridlands lies between Silversted and Joeland's Wood on the top of the Downs, near to the parish boundary.*

Kempeheld; 1440; Apuldrefield; unknown; TA {866)
OE **held**. 'The first element is probably the surname Kemp(e), derived from the OE **cempa** 'warrior', ME **kempe** 'warrior, athlete, wrestler". *See discussion in the main text on the location of this field.*

Lytill heysole, Morehaysole; 1440; Apuldrefield; unknown; TA {1161} Lower Hazel, {1140} Middle Hazel, {1139} Upper Hazel, {1142) Hazel Wood.
OE **lytel** 'little' and **māra** 'greater, bigger', OE **hæsel** 'hazel'.

Berelond; 1440; Apuldrefield; unknown; unknown
OE **bere** 'barley' + **land**

Bokerstisfiled (formerly Rd Strudell); 1440; Apuldrefield; unknown; TA {686, 689} The Buckhurst
'Buckhurst's **feld**, though whether Buckhurst is here the place-name itself or a derived surname is uncertain. Presumably Rd (Richard) Strudell is a former owner.'

Rd le Meche; 1440; Apuldrefield; unknown; unknown
'This looks like a personal name standing alone to designate ownership of the land in question ... *Rd* is again *Richard*, and *le Meche* would be a surname, probably from OE **mecca** 'companion, friend' or possibly from OE **mēce** 'sword'.'

Vuredon Wood in Westfeld; 1440; Apuldrefield; unknown; TA {639} *West field*, {625} *Little West field*
'OE **west** 'west' + **feld**. The name *Vuredon Wood* (OE **wudu**) is tricky. The second element looks like OE **dūn** 'down, hill' ... OE **furh** 'furrow, trench' looks perfectly possible, and it is well evidenced in minor names in Surrey, but it would be highly unusual to find it as the first element. *West field and Little West field together comprise only 6 acres and appear too small to also encompass a wood. They lie within a complex of open fields to the west of the Keston to Westerham road.*

P'stes Grove; 1440; Apuldrefield; unknown; uncertain
OE **prēost** 'priest' + **grāf** 'grove, wood'. Note that the first element is in the genitive singular, hence "priest's wood" rather than "priests' wood". *TA {604} is Priests Field shaw (no punctuation given), which also lies within the open field complex.*

Pettelee Croft; 1440; Apuldrefield; unknown; uncertain
OE **croft**. **Pettelee** could relate to Petley's in the adjacent parish of Downe, for which there are 14th century forms. This is perhaps more likely than two independent names deriving from OE **pytt** 'pit' + **lēah** in such close proximity. *Two Pedley names occur at TA {102} Pedley Bank and {105} Pedley Hazel – see the Mollards Wood case study in the main text.*

Petteland alias Pynchonesland; 1440:
OE **land**. *Pynchones* in the second part is surely the genitive of the surname *Pinchon*, found elsewhere in Kent.

Sabyneslond; 1440; Apuldrefield; unknown; unknown
OE **land**. 'The first element is very probably the surname *Sabin* in the genitive case, a name noted in Kent and Surrey'.

Byggynheld; 1440; Apuldrefield; unknown; unknown
OE **helde** 'slope' rather than **hyll** 'hill', with the first element OE **bēcun** 'beacon'. *See main text for a fuller discussion of this interpretation. Given the later date of this documentary source, it is suggested that this may be the same field as Helde / Hell field [218] named in 1386. It survives in TA as Biggin hill bottom {237 and 239}.*

Strydelesden; 1440; Apuldrefield; unknown; unknown
The second element is either OE **denu** 'long two-sided valley' or **denn** 'woodland pasture.
The *Strydeles-* component looks like the genitive of the apparent surname *Strudell* noted above in *Bokerstisfield (formerly Rd Strudell)*.

Wolffricheshagh; 1440; Apuldrefield; unknown; uncertain
OE *Wulfric* masculine personal name + **haga** 'hedge, enclosure'. *The term haga occurs in only four field names in Cudham, at TA {19] Shepherds Haw, {827} Alder Haw, {909} Old Haugh and {1245} Alder Haw. See main text for discussion of these places.*

Berecroft; 1440; Apuldrefield; unknown; unknown
OE **bere** 'barley' + **croft**.

Godmannyslands; 1440; Apuldrefield; unknown; uncertain
OE **land**. The first element is the surname *Go(o)dman*. Possibly survives in TA as *Go my Lands* {626}. *This last named field is also in the open field complex and abuts the West Fields and the Priests Field.*

Analysis of other field names in the Tithe Apportionments

Denge {449}: 'Here, as elsewhere, we must be cautious when proposing etymologies without earlier data, but this looks very much like a reflex of OE **dyncge** 'manured land''. *This field abutted the northern parish boundary at Leaves Green, but now lies within the Biggin Hill airfield.*

Mallwood field {99}, **Mallwood shaw** {98}, **Great Mallwood** {97}, **Little Mall wood** {94}:
An early form for this name is *Molewode* 1381, which supports derivation from OE **māl** 'bargain, law-suit, tax' + **wudu**. *See main text for a discussion of these woods.*

Manship {940}:
'(whilst) sounding a note of caution, this looks like a reflex of OE ***ge-mæ:nscipe*** 'community, communal possession', a term … not previously encountered in Kent but which occurs a couple of times in Surrey.' *This small field of only 2 acres lies within the area of Berry's Green and abuts Cooper Coomb, discussed above. Its presence underlines the analysis of Berry's Green as an area of common land.*

Pillory Hill {1039}:
An example of 'pillory' (ME **pillori**), combined with *hill*, a rare term in place-names. *A steeply sloping hill at the top of which is the junction, adjacent to the church, of the major north-south routeway in the eastern part of the parish and the only east-west routeway.*

Ridden {122}:
'Might this be the *Reden* of 1316 which Wallenberg places "in Bertrey"? (OE *****ryden**)'. *This particular field lies in the western part of the parish and lies adjacent to the area presented as a case study in the main text. It abuts the trackway leading from the Roman road to the Biggin Hill valley and may have been a noticeable clearing within a wooded landscape. Whilst not located near to the manorial place of Bertrey, it may have formed part of that manor's holdings within the valley.*

Rob Sack {387}:
'This is a common field-name in Kent, for example *Robsack, Rob Sack, Robsacks, Rob Sacks*. No explanation has ever been offered. These names look like verb + noun formations of the *Pickpocket* and *Starve Crow* type i.e. derogatory nicknames for poor land.'
The northernmost field in the parish, near to Leaves Green.

Ropes and Bells {831}:
This name possibly refers to the rents from the field being given over to provide the ropes and bells for the church. *A 2 acre plot that lies just outside the boundary of Cudham Frith. The banking here suggest that it was a woodland compartment.*

Stapleton Bank {158}:
This name is a possible candidate for one containing OE **stapol** 'post, pillar'. Many a **stapol** is a boundary marker, though the combination with OE **tūn** 'farmstead' (if this is such) might merit a

SUE HARRINGTON

different explanation. *The field is included in the case study in the main text. It lies away from the parish boundary, but might conceivably have been on the edge of a late Anglo-Saxon estate.*

Stone Rock {376}, **Stone Rock Bottom** {1151}, **8 Acre Stone Rock** {1306}, **6 Acre Stone Rock** {1303}:
'OE **stān-rocc** 'stone rock' appears in OE glosses with the meaning 'a high rock, an obelisk'. It seems to have a peculiarly south-eastern distribution … Preliminary investigation suggests that there is a possible link with early routeways, some Roman, some not.' *Stone Rock lies on the eastern slope of the Biggin Hill valley, above the trackway that connects the manors north of the Downs to the Weald. Similarly, the other three fields lie above a trackway, that leading from the lowest part of the parish at Green Street Green up to Alder Haw {827}. They are adjacent to one another along a steep-sided valley and abut the parish boundary with Downe.*

APPENDIX 3 - A GLOSSARY OF PLACE-NAME ELEMENTS RECORDED IN CUDHAM

Croft: OE **croft** – a small enclosure. When specified by a personal name, this denotes a family plot providing for the needs of a household (F)

Denn: OE **denn** – a summer pasture for use by a distant manor, commonly in Kent a Wealden woodland for the transhumant feeding of swine (E)

Frith: OE **fyrð** – a wood, a term commonly used in Downland area (E)

Haw: OE **haga** – a particularly strong type of enclosure fence found around a wooded area, or defended settlement of estate. These sometimes survive as clearly defined banks and ditches (H)

Hurst: OE **hyrst** – a wood, a term common in the later settled parts of Kent, especially in the Weald, more rarely on the Downs. It may also refer to a woodland pasture (E) or an inhabited clearing surrounded by woodland (R)

Ley: OE **lēah** – an inhabited clearing surrounded by woodland (R) or land used for woodland pasture (H)

Rede: OE ***ryde**, also Ridden: OE ***ryden**, Ryding: OE ***ryding** – an area of cleared woodland (F)

Rough: OE **rūh** - common Kentish expression denoting poor scrub (E)

Shaw: OE **sceaga** – an irregular strip of woodland left along the steep flanks of Downland valleys or around the edges of Medieval assarts (E)

Spring: OE **spring** – a woodland that has been coppiced and allowed to re-grow (E)

Stede: OE **stede** – a pasture, probably enclosed (E)

Tye: OE **tēag** – an enclosure, a term particularly used in East Surrey (F), denoted pastoral use (E)

Warren: ME **wareine** [from ONFr warenne] – originally referring to a rabbit warren, but may also denote a dense hanging woodland (E)

OE denotes Old English; ME denotes Middle English; ONFr denotes Old Northern French
Sources of interpretation of these terms are:
(E) Everitt, 1986; (F) Field, 1993; (H) Hooke, 1989; (R) Rackham, 1995

www.ingramcontent.com/pod-product-compliance
Lightning Source LLC
Chambersburg PA
CBHW051306270326
41926CB00030B/4744